Heavenly Realm Publishing
Houston, Texas

Copyright © 2014 Stephanie Franklin, Winning Together: *His Needs Matter, Her Needs Are Important.* All rights reserved.

Published By: Heavenly Realm Publishing
P. O. Box 682532, Houston, TX 77268
www.heavenlyrealmpublishing.com
Toll Free 1-866-216-0696

Printed in the United States of America

All rights reserved. No part of this book may be reproduced, stored in a retrieval system, or transmitted by any means, electronic, mechanical, photocopying, recording, or otherwise, without written permission from the author.

Scripture quotations are from the Holy Bible. All rights reserved.

ISBN—13: 9781937911-82-9   (paperback)
ISBN—13: 9781937911-84-3 (hardback)
ISBN—13: 9781937911-83-6 (ebook)

Library of Congress Cataloging-in-Publication Data: 2014919909
Stephanie Franklin
Winning Together: *His Needs Matter, Her Needs Are Important* / Stephanie Franklin

1. Religion : Christian Life - Love & Marriage—United States. 2. Family & Relationships/ Marriage & Long Term Relationships—United States. 3. Family & Relationships : Love & Romance—United States.

This book is printed on acid free paper.

Stephanie Franklin
Stephanie Franklin Ministries
www.stephaniefranklin.org
www.stephaniefranklinministries.org

Winning TOGETHER

His Needs Matter, Her Needs Are Important.

A Guide on How to Build, Rebuild and Rekindle the Fire in the Married Couple.

Stephanie Franklin, M Th.

Heavenly Realm Publishing
Houston, Texas

*For the married couple who wants to win in
every area of your marriage and relationship.*

*For the married couple raising children or have children
and wants to win in every area of your families relationship.*

*For the single couple preparing for marriage
and wants to win while getting there.*

*For those who are co-parenting and are trying to
win with working together to raise their
child or children together in separate homes.*

CONTENTS

INTRODUCTION 11

CHAPTERS:
1. The Pioneer Woman 15
2. The Pioneer Man 19
3. Dealing with In-Laws 21
4. Covenant Agreement: *The Reaction. The Response. The Building. The Rebuilding. The Connection. The Agreement.* 33
5. Knowing You: *Confidence Builder & Spending Some "You" Time* 43
6. The Heartache of an Affair: *The Healing Process* 51
7. His Needs Matter: *His Man Cave is Needed* 71
8. Her Needs Are Important: *Her Woman Cave is Needed* 91
9. If You Want the Pink Panties, You Got to Buy the Pink Panties 115
10. If You Want the Briefs, You Got to Buy the Briefs 123
11. Romantic Love Rekindles the Fire and Keeps it Burning 129
12. Relationship Builder: *Knowing What Turns Him On & Finding Out What Affection She Likes* 133
13. Fruit & Toys Are Undefiled 145
14. We Are as One: *Sex that Fulfills* 157
15. Opposites Attract 163
16. Financial Dysfunctionalism that Destroys the Vine 169
17. Relationships Matter 177
18. Fight to Make Up or Break Up? 185
19. The Popularity of Divorce: *Break the Repeating Curse* 199
20. Present But not Connected 225
21. The Pain of Infidelity—*The Healing Process* 233
22. Issue of Communication 245
23. Anger Hidden Behind Your Hands: *Breaking the Curse* 255
24. Mind Over Matter 273
25. Christ's Love for Us 287

Emotional Needs Evaluation Chart & Check 289
Her Hobbies His Hobbies Evaluation Chart & Check 292
Group Session 295

Index   309
Winning Scriptures from the Book   310

Winning TOGETHER

INTRODUCTION

As a young girl, I can remember stepping into a room full of people that was down and quiet. As I began to mingle, the atmosphere changed to brighter, blooming, and full of life and laughter. This has also happened when it came to married couples, singles, teens, troubled teens, and children. There was a time I went around unhappy couples and by the time we all departed, the couple was hugging and sharing their love again, with the words of, "I feel better" or "I love you" with a twinkle in their eyes. I then thought it must be something different about me to be able to change negative situations, relationships, bring out the best in people, and to make people who wanted to give up on life and love, to the feeling and faith to want to act better, restore, and live again.

As I have counseled and mentored, I have come to the realization that there is a constant battle to win in any relationship and in a marriage. Nobody goes into a relationship or marriage to lose—winning is the goal. If a marriage is not constantly and consistently worked on, it can become complacent to a degree of just a relationship, or just a marriage, or just my lazy husband, or just my boring wife. The husband becomes lazy and allows the wife to have her way just to keep peace or the wife keeps her mouth closed just to keep peace. Let me go deeper than that, it can go as far as to a secret life of infidelity for each person. Once the fire is gone from the relationship, nothing but dirty dark black ashes are the result of the beauty of what the marriage were meant to be when the vows were first recited and kindled.

God has used me countless times to restore and bring relationships back together; and rekindle the fire that was lost due to broken unity, loss of trust, past hurts, or unforgiveness. I have seen that it was and still is all about giving the man and the woman what he or she needs.

In *Winning Together*, I help the wife to understand that her husband's needs matter. I help the husband to understand that his wife's needs are important too, and in *"Winning Together As a Parent"*, I help the husband and wife to understand that their children's needs are together with them and not separated. They are all important and each need should not go unnoticed.

In my book, *"The Locker Room Experience"*, although my goal is to touch the life and deal with hidden areas most athletes and coaches do not deal with, there are many points I make toward the family as being an important role in the son or daughter's life. I encourage you to read it. It will change your life.

I encourage you as you read, *"Winning Together"* to rekindle the fire. Ignite love in your relationship. Restore family issues. It works. Learn how in the book.

CHAPTER 1
The Pioneer Woman

I am writing this small excerpt from my book that will be coming out soon called, *"The Pioneer Woman"*.

THE PIONEER *Woman* comes as no surprise to the woman who pans her life after God while in hot pursuit of greatness.

THE PIONEER *Woman* was derived from how the traditional Christian woman who was told to stay quiet and surely not lead—with no purpose and no promised future. Now, in this day and time, there is a new Christian woman who says different. She is a woman who has had to take the role of a leader, a provider, and a woman who cares of the things of her home and family as she follows the leading of the Lord. She now says, *"I am a Christian woman who has a purpose and a promised future."* Whether married or single, *The Pioneer Woman* is a woman who is an innovator, inventor, forerunner, developer, creator, a discoverer who will not quit nor give up until she has victoriously won; and a woman who knows her place—when to lead and when to submit.

Being *The Pioneer Woman* means, you belong to God. You are His bride. You are His maidservant, ready to reap and glean from the threshing floor. You are splendor. You are brilliant. You are glorious. You are magnificent. You are virtuous. In the Eyes of the Lord, you are all of these things. You are all that and more! You are jazzy, you are sexy, you are intellectual, you are sporty, you can be a rough-neck when need to; you are not afraid to venture out and explore the new, you don't back down—even when the going gets tough, you are all woman, you are all powerful. You are all that!

Now that you have read what a pioneer woman is, I want to give you the reality of where a real pioneer woman comes from, from a Biblical standpoint.

Millions of women miss how beautiful they really are in the eyes of God. They miss due to the lack of not being told, as they grew up into a woman—they were never told the real truth. God never intended the woman to be abused, mistreated, or thought of as a piece of meat. This is a false conception of what a woman is thought of to be.

Many women have had to take the role of the father and the mother, even when the husband was still living in the household. As I have counseled relationships, I have heard this from time and time again, *"I have had to step up and do what he's not doing or didn't do."* Unfortunately, this is the downfall of many women and have caused relationship breakdowns and breakups. It is imbalanced when the woman has to step up and be the leader over her family when the husband is living there. For this reason, many divorces have derived from this. The man knows he is out of order but he refuses to be controlled; and refuses to line up. The woman knows the household is out of order and she refuses to take orders from a lazy controlling man. This happens everyday. In many cases, it does not reach divorce, but death or physical altercation as the result. "Winning Together: *His Needs Matter, Her Needs Are Important*" *comes to help the woman know who she is as a Woman of God and as a submitted leader of her family... Read the book for more.*

CHAPTER 2
The Pioneer Man

I write this small excerpt from my book that will be coming out soon called, *"The Pioneer Man"*.

THE PIONEER **Man** comes as no surprise to the man who pans his life after God while in hot pursuit of greatness.

THE PIONEER **Man** is a man who takes the role of a leader, a provider, and a way maker as he follows the leading of the Spirit of the Lord. He knows how to lead his family. He says, *"I am a Christian man who has a purpose and a promised future."* Whether married or single, **The Pioneer Man** is a man who is an innovator, inventor, forerunner, developer, creator, and a discoverer who will not quit nor give up until he has victoriously won, with his woman and with his family.

Being **The Pioneer Man** means, you belong to God. You are His servant and ready to reap and glean from the threshing floor. You are magnificent. You are virtuous. You are a provider for yourself (if single) and for your family as God leads you. In the Eyes of the Lord, you are all of these things. You are all that and more! You are handsome, you are sexy, you are a leader, you are sporty, and you are not afraid to venture out and explore the new, you don't back down—even when the going gets tough, you are all man, you are all powerful. "Winning Together: *His Needs Matter, Her Needs Are Important*" comes to help the man know who he is as a Man of God and as a forerunning leader of his family... *Read the book for more.*

3
CHAPTER
Dealing with In-Laws

Dealing with in-laws can be quite challenging while some can be quite rewarding.

Challenging in-laws can break up a marriage real quick, whereas some bring so much torment and confusion that it leaves the married couple fussing all the time, not desiring romance, and in disillusion until break up is the best choice.

In-laws can be rewarding in the aspect of being supportive when the married couple needs them. If one of the couple's parents has deceased, the in-laws can help with fulfilling the empty void, and if one of the couple's do not have a personal relationship with their parent(s), the in-laws can help take that place.

It is satan's goal to use whomever he can to break up something beautiful from God. This is why it is so important for any relationship to stay close to God and not allow people, family, or in-law's opinion to dictate you and your spouse's relationship. You two must be determined to win, no matter what.

There are all sorts of reasons why in-laws nosing in marital relationships. Some believe the husband or wife is not the right one, some believe the husband or wife is an opportunist (looking for an opportunity financially if the husband or wife makes a lot of money, or has a high ranking position that can promote them), while others believe they are from hell and is sent to wreck their lives rather than have something prosperous and beautiful. There are some in-laws who even attempt to control the couple by getting mad if they do not do what they want them to do. There are also some in-laws that judge the husband or wife's looks, their height status—too short too tall, too heavy or too skinny in weight, bad hygiene, rotten teeth, abusive ways, big head, big feet, got too many kids, jealous of how good or how the husband or wife looks, jealous of how the husband and wife flow together, and last, they feel that they are not good enough for the husband or the wife.

While their opinions may be true, it doesn't give the parents or in-laws any right to judge him or her. If you love your spouse, that is all that matters. Most mothers are very protective over their sons and most fathers are over protective over their daughters. This can happen the other way around as well. If there is a son or boyfriend involved, they want their wife or girlfriend to be perfect to a tee. If there is a daughter or girlfriend involved, they want the husband or boyfriend to be perfect. In addition, if he or she is not, they will fight until they can get them perfect. What the mother, father, and in-laws fail to realize is, they were not perfect when they met their boyfriend, girlfriend, husband, or wife. So how can you expect so much for them?

Being over protective can cause separation with your children. I have seen cases where the mother was so protective and controlling over her only daughter and caused all kinds of friction in her newly wedded marriage, that her mission to break the marriage up did not work. However, it caused the daughter to separate herself from the mother. You can never win being controlling and mean. Your time will come when you will reap every evil thing you sowed (Galatians 6:7, Job 4:8). It is best to love and respect them no matter what.

Although in this case, the mother seemed mean, but there are cases where the mother and father or mother or father is not controlling because they are mean, they only believe that they need to be controlling because they want the best for their son or daughter and want to help them make the right choice(s). This seems acceptable, however, what the mother and father or mother or father has to realize is when your son or daughter becomes of an adult age to marry and chooses to marry, you no longer have the right to control them and their decisions. You can state your opinion if asked. But, it all comes down to the son or daughter making the right choices for themselves (Genesis 2:24). You have raised them the best you can. You have prayed over them when they were young. Now let them go and let God take care of them. There is a scripture in the Bible that says, *"train up a child in the way he (they) should go: and when he (they) is old, he (they) will not depart from it"* (Proverbs 22:6). What this scripture means is, you have raised your child or children in the right God fearing way when they were young, and now they have become an adult, you must release them to God and allow Him to guide them, mature them, and take care of them in the marriage, direction, career, job, friendships, school, or relationships they encounter. You have to be careful not to become over protective, then you may lose them verses in your eyes you were trying to help them. Do not lose focus of the fact that it is God Who is taking care of them and that you cannot control their life and the choices they make when they are adults. You must then go back to what you prayed when they were young, and trust God in every way.

Relationship battles come in some very deep situations and have scarred the husband or wife involved. There have been cases where the father has molested the daughter and is sexually attracted (incest) to the daughter and do not want her to marry, which is the reason why he has a problem with her husband (or the other way around—mother son, mother daughter, father son). There are cases where the wife is sexually attracted to the son. He reminds her of the husband she has always wanted so she holds him, and operates like his wife and he as her husband (or the other way around— mother daughter, father daughter, father son). So, once he marries, she's totally jealous and against his wife and does anything to break them up. This should not be so. There are also cases where the mother or father does not want their child to marry because it would leave them alone. This should not be so as well. The Word of God states when a man leaves his father and mother, he cleaves to his wife (Genesis 2:24). This does not mean that he or she will never see his or her parents again, it just means that he or she minds the things of his wife or her husband first then everyone afterwards.

Spirits from satan are real. They are assigned by satan and sent to destroy the marriage and family in any way he can. Read my book, *"Breaking the Power of Strongholds"* if you need more in depth study on identifying how strongholds operate in the lives of individuals, families, singles, marriages, children, youth, and in young adults. No one is exempt from the attacks of satan, however, there is protection in Jesus Christ to protect the marriage, the parents and in-laws that come to damage, and in every relationship even those who are dating toward marriage (Psalms 91).

How to Overcome In-laws and Their Opinions

There are several points I want to give you on how to overcome the attacks of in-law's opinions:

1. Do not attack them back, but identify that it is the evil one (satan) who is responsible for their attacks (2 Corinthians 10:5).
2. Refuse to receive their attacks by not entertaining their verbal or physical attacks (Ecclesiastes 5:6).
3. Come together with your spouse and pray for your parents and/or in-laws (Psalms 133:1).
4. Stay quiet and live your own life (James 1:19).

Come Together and Celebrate

It should be the goal of the married couple and the in-laws to come together and celebrate the sweet union of the marriage of their child, niece, nephew, cousin, God-son, or God-daughter. There should not be any fighting or disagreement among you. You all should strive to be peacemakers and understand that it is the mission of satan to stop and to cancel the unity among you all to a degree that you all will divide and never speak to each other again (John 10:10). In this case, you all should come together and love one another and respect that the husband or wife has made their choice of who they want, and there is nothing you can do about it but to respect it. You may ask, "How can I respect their wife or husband and they beat them all the time, or they go out every night with other women or men?" I will say, the innocent husband or wife made their decision to marry them and you have to pray for them and respect their decision to marry them. Allow God to intervene in their marriage and not you. You will only tear your relationship with your son or daughter a part, rather to draw them back to you or keep them close to you (mother, father, and/or in-laws). I have learned that no one can change anybody. Only God can change a person. I encourage you to turn them and their relationship over to God and allow Him to work it out. When you get involved in it, you make matters worse, but when God gets in it, He makes miracles of change happen. Know your place and stay in it. God moves faster when things are in order rather than through a bunch of confusion.

Scenario 1:

Ben has just proposed to Grace. Almost Grace's entire family is against them getting married. The mother and father is against Grace marrying Ben because they are against the fact that Ben is an ex-con who has turned his life around and has a job and a new life, but he does not make nearly as much as Grace does. They have sown bad seeds of lies and discord against Ben into the rest of the family and now almost all of them do not like Ben. They all have formed a false opinion about Ben that is not true. They talk against him by saying all manner of evil against him. Some have even tried to purposely lie on Ben to Grace in order that Grace will believe them and not marry him. Well, it did not work. It has made Grace shun herself a way from her mother, father and the rest of her family. Ben can't stand her mother and father, and especially his in-laws (Grace's family). He wants nothing to do with them and do not care if they do not show up for their wedding.

Ben gets mad at Grace because she does not stand up to her parents and the rest of her family. Grace encourages Ben by letting him know that she loves him and does not judge his past because they both have one. She does not care whether he makes less than she does. She loves him and does not care what they all say and think about him. She loves him and is committed to working together, and as long as he takes care of his part in which they have discussed, she has no problems. Ben feels better and kisses her in relief.

The mother calls Grace to set a time to come and talk to her about the decision she is making with Ben. Grace's father has pushed this meeting and made his wife call her. Several of the in-laws ask to come as well. Grace reluctantly talks to Ben about it and they both agree but want to make the meeting quick. This was the worst mistake of their lives.

Grace's mother and father, and about five of their in-laws show up with the worst attitudes. They can't wait to attack Grace and Ben. One of them even has the nerve to bring a Holy Bible as if it was a lie detector test. They all get into a shouting match. Ben was ready to fight and was prepared for whatever, although he had peace of mind with Grace. He and Grace's father and a couple of Grace's in-laws get into a fist fight and one of the in-laws calls the police and pressed charges against Ben and had them put him in jail because he took the first punch. Grace is crying hysterically. She yells and pleads for all of them to leave her and her life alone. Ben goes back to jail for a very long time because he provoked his parole for hitting her father and for going back to jail, which sets back their wedding.

The question is, should Grace and Ben have been living together before they were married? Should Grace marry Ben considering his past? Why did Grace and Ben agree to let the mother, father, and in-laws come over to talk about business that was not theirs? Would you marry a person if they made less than you did? Was it appropriate of Grace's parents to reject Ben because of his past and lower salary? Was it appropriate of Grace's parents and in-laws to go barging over Grace and Ben's house, expressing their opinions and initiating the fight? How could the fight have been prevented? Did bringing the Bible do any good? Do you believe Grace and Ben will get married? How long do you believe Ben will be in jail? If this were you in this situation, what would you do? How would you feel or react either as Grace or Ben, or as them both? Write your answers below and if you are in a group, talk about it with them.

_____
_____
_____
_____
_____
_____
_____
_____
_____
_____
_____
_____

4 CHAPTER

Covenant Agreement:
The Reaction. The Response.
The Building. The Rebuilding.
The Connection. The Agreement.

There is an importance to God's Covenant Agreement, and how we as the Body of Christ and partners for God's Kingdom should conduct ourselves. We are partnered with one another in order to fulfill the binding covenant on the cross.

Just as there is a covenant for the Body of Believers that operate in the Body of Christ (Church and/or Community), there is also a covenant with marriages (Hebrews 13:4). This covenant holds many standards and responsibilities to fulfill. There is the reaction, the response, the building, the rebuilding, the connection, and the agreement.

The Reaction comes in connection when things may not always go the way you planned it to go in the relationship and how your reaction would be. When you hear bad news or when your partner does something crazy, what would your reaction be? Reaction plays a big part in how you will respond and react. Your reaction should always first be calm as you deal with the matter and not begin with yelling and out of control actions.

The Response is very similar to reaction. It is how you will reply or answer to something you do and do not like or appreciate. For example, let's take what you do not like. This seems to be where most problems arise.

When you are disrespected or violated, how would you respond? Would it be physical or would it be to figure out the best way out of the negative situation as much as possible? Your response means everything as you do not allow a negative situation in your marriage and relationship to escalate into something unnecessary or serious.

Also, your words are important in how you respond verbally to keep the peace. Yelling, shouting, cursing, and using evil choice words will make matters worse. It is okay to communicate softly and quietly with one another. It is to remain with control when your spouse may raise their voice and you do not.

The Building comes when you two are fresh in marriage and are building your marriage. Marriage is much different than courting (dating). There is a deeper union and covenant between God, you, and your spouse. This is a time when you two are coming together in agreement on how you are going to operate things within your marriage. For example, who is going to pay the bills. Who is going to pay the rent. Who is going to cook and clean. Who is going to mow the yard (or hire a yard person). Who is going to take the trash out each night. Who is going to take their bath first. Who is going to get in the bathroom first in the mornings. And last, when to talk about when you two would like to start a family (have a child or children). This is the building process.

The Rebuilding comes when something has gone wrong and has disconnected you two from each other. This is called, the rebuilding. It is when you two have made a choice to come back together and work things out. While there is no perfect relationship and mistakes will happen, rebuilding is good rather than just giving up the first time mistakes are made. The unchanging covenant from God does not ever change if separation comes or fighting or disagreement comes. It is still the same and as you regard that by doing whatever it takes to save and rebuild your marriage. Many other circumstances are not mentioned and decisions may be different.

The Re-Building comes when you two have made mistakes and are re-building your relationship, lives, and family from those mistakes and moving forward. Re-building can be quite challenging if the two partners are constantly looking in the past, bringing up old past mistakes, do not want to re-build the relationship, if the two do not work together- because it is a together thing, and if the two do <u>not</u> operate like it is all about themselves. The word "self" is not located in the word "marriage", nor is "self" located in the word "relationship". Marriage and establishing a relationship for marriage can only be built on love and trust. If trust has been violated and the two partners agree to work it out, then forgiveness must be the center focal point of that re-building. You cannot re-build while living in the past. Re-building is most effective when both partners have agreed and have decided to deal with themselves, and remove anything in <u>THEMSELVES</u> that may be hindering the relationship or marriage. If this process is not handled properly, it can destroy the marriage, relationship, and even the entire family and friends who may be involved.

The Connection comes when you two are totally connected and have come together and have gotten an understanding of your places within the marriage and relationship. You are not only connected emotionally and physically, but you two are connected spiritually (Genesis 2:23). You two are as one—flesh and bone of one binding agreement.

The Agreement comes as a chain to the connection. As you two are connected, you two are in total agreement with one another. Again, knowing your places within the marriage and staying in them is key. Submitting to one another is key to a happy wholesome marriage.

Remember these six connected tools (*the reaction, the response, the building, the rebuilding, the connection, and the agreement*) are important within your marriage, knowing that the covenant and the vow you made with your spouse and God is bonding everlasting and should not be taken lightly.

Scenario 1:

Grady has just gone in his and Mary, his wife's savings and bought his mother a $500 diamond bracelet for her birthday. He did not consult with Mary before doing so. To make matters worse, he wiped out just about all of their savings that they both were saving to buy a new house. Mary is furious because Grady did not consult with her before, and because he went in their savings and took almost all of their hard earned money. Grady doesn't feel he's done anything wrong. He feels that it is his mother and that he has a right to buy his mother anything he wants at any time. It does not matter if he and Mary agree differently about spending the money. They have a huge fight and separation is the highlight of discussion.

The question is, was Grady wrong for going into their savings? Was he wrong for taking almost all of the money out of their account? Should he have consulted with Mary before doing so? Since he is the man of the house, was it necessary for him to consult with Mary before his decision was made? Should Mary have gotten mad or should she have looked over it and worked on starting over with saving more money? Should they have gotten in an argument? Should they two separate, is this that serious? Were they two in agreement? Was there covenant connection here? If this were you in this situation, what would you do? How would you feel or react? Write your answers below and if you are in a group, talk about it with them.

___

Covenant Agreement

Covenant Agreement

CHAPTER 5

Knowing You:
*Confidence Builder &
Spending Some
"You" Time*

Confidence comes with knowing who you are. If there is no confidence, knowing yourself is questioned. The relationship in a marriage works the same way. If the spouse is not confident in him or herself, knowing themselves and what keeps the relationship kindled is questioned. In most cases, this is what happens to relationships. Most people rush into a marriage by physical attraction, the amount of money one another make, and by the sweet words that are spoken or whispered in their ears. There are also cases where having a baby out of wedlock may have rushed a marriage as well.

A man needs a woman to build him up especially if he has come from a mother or father who has downed him and have abused him. When you and him got married, you as the woman could not have expected something that he could not give. He could not give you something he was not taught. He was not taught to be confident. He was not taught to know who he is. So, you cannot expect something that was and is not there from the beginning. You have come in his life to build him up in this area, not tear him down. I have heard in speaking to certain women in the past, say, *"I ain't got no time for buildin' up or raisin' no man"* or *"I need a man—a real man and not no lil' boy"*. This will almost never happen, especially in this day and time. Most men have come from battered families and have had to <u>learn</u> how to be a man and have used his first marriage or relationship to do it. When a man requires so much attention in order to build his self-confidence, this can become annoying and the woman will be forced to find some "you" time as much as possible, or she will stray away from quality time. Too much clinginess can drown the relationship. There must be a balance.

A man is typically drawn to the father as he grows from a boy to a man, if there is dysfunctionalism within the father and son's relationship, the boy will bring that dysfunctionalism in every relationship and marriage he will ever have until that dysfunctionalism is released and removed. This is why it is easy for a man to have multiple babies by many different women, get married but soon after the wedding have an affair, control the woman to get power or to stay in control even when he knows he's wrong and out of order. His thing is, *"I ain't gon' let no woman control me"*. Through these arrogant egotistical words, millions of relationships have been torn apart with either in-house separation (separated but still living together), divorce, deadly abuse, infidelity, or even custody battles. You as a man must learn that it is not about who controls who, it is about how you two can work together as one to make the best decision possible, as you two pray and lean and depend on the answer from God (Proverbs 3:5-6). Your answer or decision does not matter, it is the Will of God for every situation you and your wife may encounter that matters. God does not lead relationships that are not biblically based. Most men and women are not praying and depending on God to lead their marriages. They are too busy complaining about every negative thing they can find with the other person, rather than what is right in the other person. They are too busy complaining about what is not right in the other person, rather than dealing with what is not right in themselves.

A woman needs a man to build her up especially if she has come from a mother or father who has put her down on a constant basis and has been abused. She is a bit different from the man. Because the girl typically is drawn to the mother, if there is a dysfunctional relationship with the mother and daughter, the daughter will grow up dysfunctional and will require a lot of attention in the area of needing a lot of love and attention, confidence building and confidence (knowing who she is). Once a relationship is established, there is only a matter of time when it will hit rock bottom because these dysfunctional areas have not been released, dealt with, or taken into consideration.

As I have counseled marriages, the number one thing I have heard was, "she or he doesn't listen to me". Each person in the relationship wants to be heard. In fact, every person, whether single or married wants to be heard. However, I have found that it is far more important to listen than to be quick to voice opinions all the time.

It is hard to gain confidence in yourself when you are always around your spouse. There has to be a balance as I have stated before. There was a couple who had a problem with having quality time to spend with each other due to demanding workloads. I encourage them to make sure that every moment they have together to take advantage of that time to please each other as much as possible—to rekindle the fire over and over and over and over again. If not, the relationship will become boring, feelings will be lost, and the thrill will leave.

Below are some <u>positive and negative</u> examples of the things that couples say to each other, and how he or she come to <u>invade</u> their "you" time.

Confidence Builder:
1. You are a fat slob, you eat too much. I'm a leave you if you don't lose that weight.
2. You are a poor coach. Why can't you coach the team to a winning team?
3. You are such a big help around the house with the kids. I really appreciate you. Can you help more?

Spending Some "You" Time:
1. Hey babe, can you iron my shirt, got a meeting at work?
2. Hey wanna' go with me, some of the other couples are meeting at a restaurant for a group dinner date?

3. Hey, can you keep our daughter Cindy for the weekend while we go out of town?

These types of examples come to invade the space of couples, some in a negative way, and some in a positive way. If you are guilty with either one or more of these points, I encourage you to make it your goal to be as positive with your spouse as much as possible and respect their "you" time as much as you can.

Scenario 1:

Lacey longs to spend some "you" time alone. However, with her controlling and demanding husband, the kids, and keeping other family member's kids, it is impossible. Her husband John is lazy and does not want to do anything, he waits on Lacey hand and foot. Making her do everything and when she even look like she wants her "you" time, he invades it by coming against it and either make her fix him some food or by making her clean the house again and again. The kids yells and demands for her to play with them and fix them snacks. The other family member's kids complain and want their way. So her "you" time is hindered and she is a slave to everyone's selfish desires of making her do everything for them.

The question is, why is the demands all on her? Why doesn't John have any chores or accountabilities? Why is she keeping her family member's kids, is this a hindrance or a help? Is John controlling or acting as a husband and father should? Does John want to see Lacey happy and have time for herself? Why doesn't Lacey talk to John and tell him how she feels instead of doing everything he asks? Is it her responsibility to see about the kids alone and take care of their wants and needs alone? Is it John's responsibility as well? Should John be held responsible to spend some quality time with Lacey? If this were you in this situation, what would you do? How would you feel or react? Write your answers below and if you are in a group, talk about it with them.

_____
_____
_____
_____
_____
_____
_____
_____
_____
_____

Knowing You

CHAPTER 6

The Heartache of an Affair:
The Healing Process

Affairs occur all across the world on a daily basis. The most hurtful thing about a supposedly successful relationship is when the spouse has an affair. Most marriages almost never recover from this heartache. If the trust factor is broken, the relationship is lost and the guilty one who is responsible, has to work overtime in order to win his or her marriage back with the hope of forgiveness. I have encountered where the spouse who committed adultery either never came back because they did not want to, fear of trusting again, or because the thought of what they did hurts too bad. They are happy with their estranged lover and the thought of restoring the marriage is out of the question.

The heartache of an affair comes with a price. I have seen cases on the news where the wife caught the husband in the act with another woman, and the wife killed both the husband and the lover who he or she was having sex with. This is the tragic heartache of an affair. I have also heard of cases where the husband walked out on the marriage with another woman and later the wife finds out and confronts him; afterwards still wants to rekindle the marriage but the exception the husband has is that he wants both—the lover and the wife. Like they say, "you can't have your cake and eat it too". You cannot have both pieces of the pie. You must chose who you want. Before a vow is made, you should think about whether or not marriage is for you rather than to get in it, and pull out in a nasty way that could cost you your life or hurt the one involved.

Why Do Affairs Happen?
Many affairs happen in many different cases. Below are some reasons:
- There are times when violation occurs, when one of the spouses have been raped and abused as a child and sex is hard for them to cope with, with their spouse.
- Not having sex regularly.
- Infidelity.
- Rape within the marriage.
- Physical abuse.
- Mental and verbal abuse.
- Hardship with finances.

- Spouse makes more money.
- Fight for constant control.
- Daily workload.
- Lack of love and affection.
- Lack of sex at all.
- Lack of communication.
- Lack of attention.
- Lack of trust.
- Lack of love, affection, and romance.
- No laughter and fun quality time.
- No quality time spent, or romantic quality time spent.
- Constant stubborn and selfishness.
- Constant complaining and nagging.
- Constant picking, fighting and bickering.
- Never happy or satisfied.
- Self-centered: Want their way all the time.
- Terminal Illness.
- Too much weight gain.
- Too little in weight.
- Constant hygiene problem.
- Unclean—does not take baths.
- Too many people involved in the marriage and relationship.
- Spends too much time living in the past.
- Constantly brings up what they did wrong.
- Constantly brings up what they did in the past.

- Unforgiveness: refuse to release the hurt from the past.
- Negative and constantly puts one another down.
- Not willing to work together.
- Puts the child or children before the spouse.
- Spends all of their time with the child or children and none with the spouse.
- Works too much, hardly ever see each other.
- Career differences.
- Not compatible and do not choose to try to be. Married for the wrong reasons.
- Pride, no one wants to listen or change their ways.

No one wants to come home to any of these bullets above. Nor does anyone want to experience this within his or her marriage. There can never be a union between the husband and the wife if these examples are involved. Also, if there are children involved, they do not want to be a part of this as well.

How Do I Keep Affairs Away?

Meeting the needs of your spouse will keep away affairs. It is a must to make sure that their needs are met and this is your number one priority. Constantly rekindling the fire by staying romantic and spontaneous on a daily basis—finding new ways to please your spouse is another one. It will also work with constant prayers and praying together. Having a great marriage is not always so religious and deep. Although it is important that God is in the relationship, He does not want you to overdo it where you lose the sense of the beauty of sex and romance that He gave for you two to share.

Pay close attention to how you come off, and constantly nagging about the past. Never satisfied and ready to tear your spouse down rather than build him or her up will help keep infidelity away. You do not see the good in your spouse, but always seeing the bad and magnifying the bad to make them feel bad and embarrassed.

Do not play with fire. Men and women flirt all the time especially when there is a weakness noticed. They may flirt with their eyes, body, mouth, or by actions. Do not play with fire especially if you are already weak in that area. You must put the fire out before it ever gets started. You put it out by not giving attention to it. Remove yourself from the environment. For example, if an attractive woman walks by you with a coke bottle figure and is really catching your eye, you must quickly turn your head and walk off or leave. You have to do whatever you need to do <u>not</u> to entertain the picture that is before you. I have heard some say, *"its ok to look as long as you don't touch"*. I disagree with this statement. It is not ok to look because when you look, you look too long, then the connection has a chance to connect. Once the connection connects, it's almost no turning away. Most men are the aggressors, so they will move first. However, this is not always the case. Now a days, the woman moves first especially if there is a connection and a vibe that is unbearable. She will make the first move no matter if married or not. But, once you open the door and make yourself available as if to want what is before you, your prize will be just what it is and once you get the prize, and after the damage is done, it may not be what you thought it was going to be; and then it is almost no turning back afterwards. Lives change. People get hurt. Families are destroyed. Unnecessary deaths or injuries are the result. Strongholds are responsible for this fight. However, they can be pulled down and broken, and brought under the obedience of the Will of God.

> *"For the weapons of our warfare are not carnal, but mighty to the pulling down of strongholds."*
> **2 Corinthians 10:4**

> *"Casting down imaginations, and every high thing exalteth itself against the knowledge of God, and bringing into captivity every thought to the obedience of Christ;"*
> **2 Corinthians 10:5**

The damage is not done by the hurt, it is done by the demonic stronghold that is within the person that is almost never detected in the lives of many before it is too late. Once the stronghold you are dealing with is recognized, you can begin to renounce (reject/rebuke) it and get the victory over it through prayer, fasting, and release.

    Know when to give and take. Know when to talk and when to shut up. Know when to say yes and when to say no. It is not your way all the time. There are times when you two have to agree to disagree. You two are in a marriage and will not always agree on everything, so, to come to a common agreement like, "ok I understand, I do not agree but I understand how you feel". This will lead to a lifetime of a good, unselfish, understanding, peacemaking relationship.

How to Heal From an Affair

This is a narrow path to follow in terms of a relationship where infidelity has invaded the marriage. In most cases the relationship is never rekindled, but if it was going to be rekindled and in order for healing to find its way in, this is what would need to happen,

1.	Both should turn to God (Exodus 20:14).
2.	Make sure the spouse who is guilty tell the honest truth.
3.	Make sure that the affair with the other party is completely over.
4.	Make sure you open yourself completely and honestly up to your spouse. Tell everything. Spare not the rod. Do not hide anything, even if it is unbearably nasty or embarrassing. If you do not choose to save your marriage and heal from it, then these steps are not necessary because they will not be effective anyway.
5.	You must forgive if you are the innocent one involved (Matthew 18:21-22).

6.	Seek counseling, and prayerfully come together and seek God and allow Him to heal and rekindle and bring back the husband or wife you married in the beginning.
7.	Allow time to take its course. Do not rush healing. Healing cannot be rushed. Each person is different. Therefore, healing is a process that happens differently by each person or relationship.

Pick Up the Broken Glass Pieces

Within every antagonizing disagreement, disappointment, and letdown, there are broken feelings, disappointments, failures, guilt, and suicidal thoughts that are shattered all over the place. They have come as distractions. Most are small pieces that have turned into large pieces because you did not resolve the conflict of the affair, or did not do it quick enough. You allowed it to escalate and more pieces fell and shattered until they all piled up on top of each other until a point where you or they exploded. You cannot live in the past or thrive on being phony or hypocritical just to keep peace, and are either still burning up inside or is still hurting inside.

I encourage you to pick up the broken pieces in your life and marriage.

1. You should quietly and peacefully talk about what it is that is bothering you or what you are hurting about to your spouse, the one that has hurt you, made you angry, and move on.

2. The devil wants you to hold all of that hurt, anger, and pain on the inside and never get it out. Do not allow the devil to defeat you, your freedom within, nor your relationship.

3. You have chosen to forgive him or her and have chosen to stay and work it out. Now you need to pick up the broken pieces if you have to do it or them one by one until you get it or them all out and release them all.

4. Then move on by not bringing it or them back up, slamming it in their face again and again, reminding them every chance you get, shutting down and shutting yourself out, or closing yourself up in a closet or a box.

5. It has already happened, whether it is you as the guilty person or as the victim. Now pick yourself up and move on by canceling conflict completely out of your life and marriage. I say, by the strips of Jesus Christ you are healed from every wound and every scar from your painful past (Isaiah 53:4-5).

Do Not Take Your Marriage for Granted

Taking your marriage for granted will result in selfishness and pride, seeing things only your way, wanting your way all the time, not appreciating him or her; and especially after they have done something special and are always trying to win with you. You can close the door to any relationship by doing this. When you look around, he or she has found someone else that fills the empty void you lack to fulfill. It is important to always please you last. Pleasing your spouse first will always keep the knot tight in your relationship—realizing it is not always about you.

Scenario 1:

Cindy loves John. Nothing and no one could come between their love for one another. Cindy is so submitted and committed to John. She knows her place as a wife. She knows how to please him in every area of their marriage. But John somehow still is not happy. In fact, he finds himself sneaking out to a local strip club in the arms of another woman to find pleasure and a lap dance. All the while he tells Cindy he's going over a friend's house only to run in the arms of other women.

It is now going on a year and Cindy notices that John seems different and withdrawn, especially when they are sexually and romantically involved. John does not last long, he does not four play—jumps right into it with no feeling of love toward Cindy at all, and his words are silent. Cindy begins to feel violated as if she is making love to someone else other than the spouse she fell in love with.

It is obvious that Cindy is innocent. She's done nothing wrong. John is obviously the guilty one. However, the question is, why did John go outside of his marriage? Why did he feel as if he had to find fulfillment outside of his marriage? What drew him to the strip club? What drew him away from his wife that fulfilled his every need? Was Cindy too good to John? Did John take Cindy for granted? What are your thoughts on this and how would you have handled this scenario if it were you? Write your answers below and if you are in a group, talk about it with them.

_____
_____
_____
_____
_____
_____
_____
_____
_____
_____
_____
_____
_____
_____
_____
_____
_____
_____
_____

Scenario 2:

Rachel is always at church. She is very committed to the church and nothing can keep her from it. In fact, she is there way after hours—morning, noon, and during night services. All the while she is constantly praying that her unsaved husband, Jeff is the man that God wants him to be.

Her midnight romantic moods have become a turn off because she hasn't been there all day and the force of her selfish needs pushes him to sleep on the couch.

Jeff, hard at work at his 9 to 5 manufacturing job likes to eat lunch in the lobby instead of running out for lunch like all the other co-workers do. A beautiful woman walks up *and asks if she can sit and eat at his table because there are no other tables available. He quickly agrees as his mind flashes to his wife, whom he still loves very much although she's never home to fulfill his needs. He remembers how beautiful she was when he first laid eyes on her when they first met.*

Jeff and the beautiful woman's conversation begin with small talk, which found to be very compatible, about the job and their individual positions into an early dinner date.

They couldn't wait to see each other. In fact, they enjoyed their conversations from earlier that day so much that a second date came so soon. After that, the dates became more and more, day by day, until meeting at a local hotel was the next step.

They meet at a local hotel and found that their love was a connection and could not keep them from each other's arms. They never wanted to depart. The thoughts of Rachel never crossed Jeff's mind. He was in Heaven with his co-worker. She paid so much attention to him, she spent time with him, she listened to him, and she met his sexual needs. She was the woman he had always dreamed of in Rachel.

Rachel, on the other end, still praying, never noticed that Jeff was being unfaithful until she came home one late night from church and Jeff still had fresh cologne on his body as if he'd just came in right before her. Rachel begins to question Jeff. She begins to tell Jeff how good he smelt and questioned if he'd just come in right before she did. He quickly replied no and that he didn't appreciate her questioning him.

The questions became interrogating. Jeff begins to feel convicted for what he had done in-so-that he had to admit that he was committing adultery with another woman and that he was moving out. Rachel was devastated. She had believed God for her marriage and it was like a ton of bricks went down her throat. She never expected, although she never tried to meet his needs either. Her needs were more important. It was good that she went to church and believed, but she did not use her faith in the natural to win her husband by inviting him to church, or to please him in every way so that would possibly draw him to want to meet her needs and draw close to God. She was blind and selfish and did not even realize it. Now her husband has committed himself to another woman and there is nothing she can do about it.

Jeff moved out and committed himself with the other woman for over 6 months. Rachel called him everyday until he changed his number.

One day Jeff finally broke down and told the other woman that he loved her but was still in love with Rachel.

He eventually called Rachel back and went back to her house to work things out with her.

Rachel never apologized for her faults but asked Jeff why he cheated on her. Jeff began to pour out in anger by telling her that he was tired of being alone and not having his needs met, and that he got tired of her always being at the church. He also mentioned that he might have gone with her but she never asked and acted as if she didn't need him.

Rachel broke down crying and began to tell Jeff that she was sorry, that she didn't see it that way, and that she will try to do better if he moves back with her. Jeff listened but was still hurt and let Rachel know that he loved the other woman and have since let her know that he was madly in love with Rachel and that he could no longer be with her. However, he didn't want to be with either one. They are working things out day-by-day; maybe in the future they can be together.

The question is, why didn't Rachel see that her husband could not get where he needed to be spiritually if she never invited him to church? Why didn't Rachel see that she was not fulfilling her husband's needs by coming in late at night when he was tired from work and she had not been there all day and night? She was not available to love him, listen to him, or even act as if she wanted to help draw him closer to God and the church? Why didn't Jeff just say how he felt before stepping out on his wife? Why didn't Jeff just ask to go to church with Rachel? Why didn't Jeff do something romantic to change the way he felt about his wife sexually? Why didn't they choose to see a counselor to work things out? Was it Rachel's or Jeff's fault that Jeff stepped out on their marriage? What are your thoughts on this? How would you have handled this scenario if it were you, and if you were Rachel or Jeff, or them both? Write it below and if you are in a group, talk about it with them.

The Heartache of an Affair

CHAPTER 7
His Needs Matter

His Man Cave is Needed

H**is needs matters.** There are many times when meeting the needs of the man is over looked. Men have needs too. The stereo type that the world draws to is a man's only needs are sex. This is not always the case. A man has needs just as the woman does. In fact, his needs are just as demanding as hers are.

A man wants more than just a rub down and a hot fulfillment from his spouse at night. There are times when he wants to be appreciated, verbally loved, and made to feel strong.

Appreciation is the Key to His Needs

When the man is appreciated, he feels needed and this draws him to do more things. Appreciation comes in different ways. It may come in a verbal jester of:

1. "Honey, I appreciate you taking out the trash." Or,
2. "Thank you for washing the car, you are so sweet." Or,
3. "I appreciate how you took the kids out and gave me a rest, I'm going to do something special for you." Or,
4. "Babe you look so handsome, I love the cologne you have on." Or,
5. "I love you so much sweetheart, you are the best husband in the world. Thank you for being you." Or,
6. "I have planned a dinner for two on the beach to show my appreciation of the hard work you put in to making me happy." Or,
7. "I have surprised you with a candle light dinner. I appreciate you so much." Or,
8. "I have planned a picnic at the park, I want to please you in every way." Or,
9. "Thank you for buying this new dress, I love it!" And so on.

You appreciate him without adding something negative at the end of the positive jester. If you do this, your jester will turn into a fight instead of a memorable, special positive, loving moment for him.

He needs to hear positive things from you, not negative and always complaining about what he cannot and do not do. If you appreciate him and stop complaining, this will help with his change and will convict him to do the same back to you.

You May Want to Show Physical Jesters Like:	
Appreciation	**Affection**
1. Hold his hand when in public →	Kiss him at times while holding hands
2. Thank him for cooking →	Treat him to a candle light dinner
3. Give him a loving card that says how special he is →	Run him a nice hot bath and rub him down
4. Take him for ice cream just because →	Verbally tell him how awesome he is and how much you love him

Good Hygiene

As your mate he wants to show you off every chance he gets. So good hygiene is important to not only turn him on to want to please you, but it also helps when pleasing with passionate sex is going forward. It is embarrassing when hygiene is the negative factor when you and him are out in public or are invited to a gathering. Good hygiene matters if you want to keep the fire burning in your marriage and relationship. It is a complete turn off when bad hygiene and bad breath keeps his needs from being met because he can't stand to get close to you.

Good Looks Matter

Most women like to shop so it does not take much to get a woman in a store to shop to look good not only for herself, but also for her spouse. Just as she loves to shop, getting her hair, nails, and toes done comes right in line.

Men love when a woman looks like a woman. They love when a woman smells like a woman. So pay close attention to how you smell and how you look. It is good to find a hairstyle he likes as well as nails that are not off the wall, along with toes that are too smelly and scaly to be touched, massaged, or kissed. Men like to tease, and what a terrible thing when he is turned off because of these imbalances. His needs matter.

Verbally Loved
Reaching out with a simple "I love you" on a daily basis removes weights that may have accumulated throughout the day for you and him. Sometimes all a man wants to hear is "Babe, I love you" rather than "do you have any money? Why you always broke?" "Where my money you owe me?" In most cases, this is over looked because of the role of the leadership that the husband is to play with his wife, kids (if any), and household. The wife tends to get caught up in the daily needs of the house, rather than verbally appreciating what has already been done or getting done at the time. Time taken to do this will result in a better husband and loving husband, and he will then turn and do the same back to you. A transformation will occur for the both of you.

Made to Feel Strong
As I have mentioned in the paragraph above "Verbally Loved", due to the leadership role the man has to play in the household, there are times when he is not made to feel strong when it comes to the wife's verbal

jesters, disagreements, and judgmental let downs. You as the wife must make your husband feel strong at all times, never weak. Build him up where he's been torn down. Do not add fuel to his fire he's having on that particular day. He already has enough on him and he needs your help with being positive, and keeping him lifted up. If this is a no win for you as a wife, stay quiet, pray, and allow him to come forward until you see a way to get inside and encourage.

I realize there are some women who would disagree when it comes to making the man feel strong. However, you must understand that God designed men to be strong and to take charge over their household. <u>Not</u> egotistically <u>control</u>, but to lead the household as you as the wife and him come together and seek God together for the best decisions for your marriage, family, and household.

Both of you cannot be strong and aggressive at the same. One must submit while the other stands strong in leadership. This is always appropriate with the man being the leader and strong, while the wife is submitted and sensitive to his needs. Again, there is to be no egotistical control over the wife, but leadership. There is a difference. Control leads to abuse, leadership leads to Godly decisions made for the both of you and your family.

As I have counseled with families and marriages, the men almost have said the same thing, "she doesn't make me feel like a man", or "always putting me down like I'm the only one wrong", or "she never admits her faults", or "she doesn't listen to me", or "her way or no way", or "she never shuts up", or "she won't let the past go", or "she spends way too much money and then blames it on me when we don't have enough money to pay bills," or "she won't give it up when she's mad". These are some common jesters but they each are jesters to take notice of if you are a wife and want to be a better wife and to better your marriage. It should be your goal to win in marriage and not to give up and become lazy and defeated. Marriage should be something beautiful between a man and woman, not grievous.

If you as the wife are the breadwinner, this can cause a problem in the marriage whereas the husband does not feel strong if you are always nagging him about money issues, or bragging about how much more money you make and his is just an add on. These kinds of jesters are not acceptable and must be stopped if you want to continue to have a healthy loving relationship. I do not know no man that would put up with that for long. It is already eating him up that he cannot provide for you like you provide for him. A good way to remember and put away with this type of behavior is to be reminded that you two are **ONE**. You are to work together and seek God for the final answer on everything.

Terminate financial comments that hinder your relationship from moving forward. Everything else is not going right why remind your spouse of what he already knows to be true? He is doing the best he can and needs you to look at what he is giving and not what you want him to give, especially if that is all he has. One thing that can kill a marriage is fussing over money and debt. If you are in a better position than he is in terms of finances, you should help him by working together to pay off he debts he has as well as you have. Not just yours and laughing and taunting him because he is not as financially stable as you are.

Admitting your faults along with him, allows him to see that he is not the only one who needs to change his negative ways. There is no perfect relationship. In fact, there is no one sided relationship where one person is wrong all the time. You both have your share at being wrong at times. With that said, you as his wife should never act as if you're picture perfect and all the blame and wrong is on him. Most times, you can quickly turn the mirror you're holding up toward him, back toward you and find so many imperfections that will keep the mirror on you for a life time. No one is in position to judge. This not only goes for other outside relationships, but the very one you are in as well.

How to Spark His Flames

Men love to love. In fact, they love to love more than be loved simply because they are the givers. They love to please, and as a result, most times never get pleased back. They release and the woman receives. She is not the giver, she is the receiver. However, there are times when the man's needs are to be loved. He at times want to receive and not give all the time. This sparks his flames. In this area, the woman should pay close attention to him and watch and study to see exactly what he wants at that moment and see what turns him on. You are not caught up in self at that moment. It is not your needs that are important, it is his needs that matter. You are all about meeting his needs. Your goal should be to take care of him whether sexually, passionately, affectionately, verbally, mentally, emotionally, and spiritually.

Needs are different for each couple. So, this is why I made the point that you should watch your partner and see what his needs and desires are at that moment. This is not always sexual. This is also conversational, emotional, affectionate, romantic, comical, a listening ear, just relaxing together with nothing said, just caressing one another, or just enjoying one another's presence. There are times when women can talk too much. You ruin the mood because you want what you want, not caring or thinking about pleasing him. Some men may not admit it, but that is a pet peeve. They hate that. It bothers them, but they may not admit it because they don't want your answer to be no when they are ready to be pleased later in the bed. So, they go along with it just to get their pleasure any way they can.

I encourage you as a female to rest and allow silence to be the conversation, and rest in each other's arms. There is nothing more beautiful to be in the arms of a loving, strong man wrapped around you. Take advantage of the moment.

You cannot change a man, and a man cannot control a woman. It is important for you as a woman to let your man be a man. If he just lost his job, and is out of work for several months, don't curse or nag him. Do not keep reminding him that he is unemployed and lazy and need to find a job, and certainly do not go and find one for him. You may go and find one with him. Let a man feel like a man. I am not saying to build his ego by allowing him to control your conversation as to make you say all good things about him and his current situation. I am saying to build him up in prayer, fasting, and in the Word of God (Bible). And, build him up with kind words that make him feel encouraged and that he can faithfully get out there and get his life back and his career back. You never know you may fall in the same situation he's in and will need his strength, encouragement, love, and spiritual help.

If loving your husband is hard, most times it is due to hurt, unhappiness—wasn't what you expected, doesn't turn you on, is not romantic, abusive, etc. I have seen cases where the husband was the perfect man and the wife just could not love and please him like he needed to be loved and pleased. She was dealing with past issues within herself that stopped her from reaching out and feeling affectionate enough to show it to him. As a result, the relationship eventually deteriorated with the worst shocking conclusion of infidelity.

Generational curses from the parent or down the bloodline will have an effect on your marriage if you do not pray and seek God for deliverance. For example, if the wife has come from a molested, abusive home, she may be withdrawn from the husband. As a result, she may not kiss you when you get home or before bedtime. She may not have a desire to make love. She may turn away when you're trying to turn her on physically. She may yell at you when you buy her yellow roses as oppose to red roses—never satisfied. She may even lash out at you for no reason. She may even not say a word. Squeezing a word out of her is like squeezing an over ripped orange.

When you do not love your husband and say all manner of evil like cursing him out every chance you get, got to get the last word, try to think of every negative word or jester to tear him down, is a hateful unhappy person. One thing that disturbs me to see is hateful women with loving good men. And vice versa, a hateful man with a loving good woman. They always say, a good man is hard to find and a good woman is hard to find. You can literally ask yourself, "Am I a good woman or a hateful woman?" Which one would you answer to? Hopefully to a loving woman. Explain why below.

_____
_____
_____
_____
_____
_____
_____
_____

<u>Communication is the Key to Every Winning Together Relationship.</u> It is the key when it is shared truthfully. No matter what is shared. An example is listed below:

> ***<u>From the Female Point of View:</u>*** "I hate it when you pee on the toilet seat and leave it there, do not let the toilet seat

down when you're done, but I do like it when you rub my feet and talk sexy to me."

From the Male Point of View: "I hate it when you nag about everything, do not brush your teeth but want to kiss all the time, fart while holding me romantically, but I like it when you tell me what I do that makes you happy and not complain."

If you two want to win, there must be truthful communication and respect to make changes to areas your spouse is not happy with.

Respect His Man Cave:
Most men want a man cave. Very few I have spoken to say different. I realize as a woman, it may seem unnecessary to you as his partner because he has you and you ask why would he need anything else but me all day in every way? Well, I hate to hurt your feelings but everybody needs their space. Everyone needs "me" time. You are not the only one that exists. I think if you would really think about it, you would agree for yourself. Getting with the girls ever so often don't hurt. You need that time away, which allows you and him some space, time to miss one another, and brings a since of freedom and respect. This leaves room for you to go out with girlfriends and go out with the kids or go visit your parents. Occupy your time while he is enjoying his time. Your time will come.

This temporary separation does not bring grounds for you two to get back together and speak negative of all the fellas who came to your man cave gathering. It is a time to come back together and make him feel like his time and space was just as important to you, and vice versa. He does not want you coming to him and talking about what your day was like or how many errands you had to run. That is selfish. At this time, it is all about him. Trust me, I know you are saying as a female that is way over board and that you should be able to share about you too. No, I still stand on what I am saying, at that moment, it is not about you, it is all about him. You come later.

A man cave is not always a meeting, party, or socially gathering in a room with all the guys, it is also a place where he can get away and get a breather, clear his head on some things, or just relax alone. You as his partner must respect this and it is not an option, especially if you want your marriage or relationship to continue to be strong and full of love. It is something about time away that brings release, recuperation, and equal partnership.

A man cave may be located in different places:
1. A basement
2. A garage
3. A guest room or room other than the master bedroom you and her share
4. Covered patio *(preferably in the back yard)*
5. A tree house
6. The guest house

I have provided some scenarios in which women say toward their husband having a man cave:

Scenario 1:

My husband and I had been very romantic from the time we made our wedding official. We love being together and spend very little time being a part. His birthday is coming up and I wonder what could I get him because he seem to have everything.

I searched and searched but could not find anything that I thought would please him. So I gave up.

A few days before his birthday, I asked him what he wanted which got me nowhere because he didn't even know. It wasn't until a day before his birthday that he came to me with a newspaper and pointed to an article about a "man cave". He said, "this is what I want." Of course, it took me by surprise. I never thought in my wildest dreams that he would want such a thing but as I began to think about it, he has a stressful job, he likes to read alone sometimes, and often have his brother and friends over for some hangout talks out by the cars in the driveway. At first I wanted to be selfish, thinking only of myself as to the fact of what he need with a man cave, he has me? And I also thought, if he gets a man cave, he won't want to spend time with me—his man cave is all he would want.

In thinking about this, hoping he didn't see the change in my facial expression, I agreed and said, "I think that'll be a good idea." His face lit up, and I later received gifts; and it wasn't even my birthday. I even got a romantic bath. So I believe if a wife would put aside her feelings and realize that every man needs his space, understand that it would only relieve stress and create a since of personal space, help bring a since of freedom in which allows him to be nothing but a man; and it would help bring the relationship closer and more respectful. It was rewarding to me, and I'm glad I agreed.

He chose the garage as his man cave and of course, he did not want me to help him clean it out and decorate it. I smiled and understood.

The next scenario is not so understanding. In fact, this relationship almost broke up because of lack of agreement:

Scenario 2:

My husband and I have three boys and I am the only woman in the house. They all teamed up on me about me letting them have their own man cave. It was like a barbarian bunch of men teaming up on the little ol' lady. I immediately got offended. We fussed all night and all day the next day. My husband could not seem to understand that he did not need a man cave with his fourteen, fifteen, and sixteen year old boys. He felt that I was being way over board and controlling and stated, "every man needs his space. It will be good for the boys and I." To top it off, one of my boys yells, "yea mom, stop hated!" I almost broke into tears, but fought back and gave them a good tongue-lashing and something worse than a man cave.

Later my husband did not agree with my horrible attitude and discipline with the boys, and became very angry and argued that if he couldn't have his alone time, he was going to move out, but quickly changed his mind for the sake of the boys. He instead stated that he was not going to sleep in the same bed until I agreed. The result is, he's having cold nights on the couch. We did not agree and that immediately changed our relationship. I'm still coping with that idea that he thinks young boys can share a man cave with other grown men and think that's alright.

This last scenario is one that may seem off the wall, but is true in most homes as most will not admit it:

Scenario 3:

My husband and I just moved into a new city and just hired a realtor to help us look for a new home. It did not take long for our realtor to find the perfect home. As we walked from room to room, from the front door to the back yard, I was hooked but my husband was not. He asked the realtor, "is this all to the house?" The realtor quickly responded that there was one more room left to see. As we entered this very large room, which was way away from the rest of the house, my husband quickly yells, "Now I'm satisfied! I love it!" The realtor and I both bewilderedly stared at each other as my husband yells again, "perfect for my man cave!" I quickly threw in, "who said this was going to be a man cave, you don't need a man cave?" He throws out, "I gotta' have my space." I felt that he did not need a man cave because I heard negative things about a man having his own man cave but was willing because I understand space is important for our relationship. The only flaw that made me upset was the stripper pole in the middle of the room. That really concerned me. It was obvious that he didn't have any problems with it, in fact, he goes over and jumps up and straddles the pole and slowly slides down as he smiled saying, "this brings great ideas," He had the nerve to twitch his eye brows and smile at me romantically. I wanted to get mad but smiled instead and returned with, "you are so nasty."

It is important to communicate and come to an agreement with your spouse especially on scenarios like these just stated. It can have its negative feedback instead of rewards if you two do not communicate and do not look at it in a selfish way as your opinions only matters.

Below are some questions you and your partner or a group can talk about concerning having a man cave:

Do you think the wife should be allowed in the husband's man cave? Why? Why not?

_____
_____
_____
_____
_____
_____
_____
_____
_____
_____

Why do you need a man cave?

_____
_____
_____
_____
_____
_____
_____
_____
_____
_____
_____

Should you and your wife have a man cave together? Why? Why not?

Should the wife control how the man cave looks? Why? Why not?

Should your wife control who to invite to your man cave? Why? Why not?

Should the kids hang out in the man cave? Why? Why not?

What are your thoughts on each scenario? State them below for personal use and for group discussion.

CHAPTER 8
Her Needs Are Important

Her Woman Cave is Needed

H**er needs are important.** Just as the man has needs that matter, the woman has needs that are just as important and cannot be overlooked; and if you as her husband want the marriage and relationship to flourish. I have heard that you cannot blame a man or a woman from loving you and wanting you. It is his or her feelings and they cannot be changed unless you neglect, reject, or hurt them. Love, trust, and respect is a <u>MUST</u> factor.

Women are quite different than men when it comes to pleasure and what's important to her. Her pleasure is much more intense than that of a man. He is in and out, she is hold me and make it last. There is much more attention and emotion that has to be given to the woman. The woman was created that way. I am reminded of a passage of scripture in Genesis 2:18, where woman was made for man and that God made woman for man. Also, in verse 22-24 it speaks of woman being made from man's rib and his bone is her bone and her flesh is his flesh, which means that they two are one. What this means is that they two are to work together in making sure one another is pleased in every way. I share that point to say that just as it is important to fulfill the man's needs, it is also to fulfill the woman's needs; and to know that they both are important and they both matter.

Just as it doesn't take much to satisfy the needs of a man as you two make love, it is important to know while you two are making love that her needs are important and they are much more intense. Like holding her, caressing her, taking your time with her, softly speaking sweet loving words to her; and showing her how much she means to you and you to her.

Appreciation is the Key to Her Needs Being Important
When a woman is appreciated, she opens herself up more to him. She invites him in instead of cautiously watching him and closing him out. Appreciation comes in ways of verbally telling her you love her, bringing flowers occasionally when it is not a holiday, taking or having flowers or candy delivered to her job, kissing her and caressing her back in your quiet time, and making gestures of appreciation like, "honey, thank you for the great dinner you cooked, it was great." Or, "thank you for taking care of the kids, I'm so lucky to have you as my wife." Or, "you look

stunning and your hair is beautiful." Or, "I've set up a candle light dinner for two." Or, "I've made reservations for us to go out on a romantic boat ride." These are the appreciations that your wife needs. A Woman loves it when a man tells her that he loves her and mean it. It is meaningful when you verbally tell your spouse, but more meaningful when you show it.

As I have stated in the last chapter but the other way around, it is important that you as her man appreciate her without adding negative comments right after the positive jesters. Your negative jesters will turn into a fight and into a negative memorable moment instead of a positive one. Who wants a nasty fight after something romantic? That just kills what could be a special lasting moment for eternity. Yes, I said eternity. Unbelievably your wife remembers your sweet words years and even decades from now, even when you might not think anything of them. Most women remember decades back like your wedding, anniversary, romantic nights and trips, when you acknowledged the things she likes, favorite color, whereas most men struggle. So, make sure your words are always words that bring love, compassion, uplifting, and strength, rather the opposite.

On a bad day, she needs your positivity. Your complaining will only drive her to shut down completely, shun away from your affection, push herself out of the house by coming home late, spending late hours at work and leaving you with a filthy home, hanging out with uninvited friends, or even into another man's arms. Constantly complaining about everything and making unnecessary comments like, "you cook steak when you should have cook chicken." Also complaining about what she did not do rather than what she did do—never satisfied. If you appreciate her and let her know she's important too, I can assure you, this will help with areas that may not be right in her and will encourage and convict her to change and do the same back to you.

The chart below shows when appreciation is given, affection comes:

You May Want to Show Physical Jesters Like:	
Appreciation	**Affection**
1. Hold her hand when in public	→ Kiss her, hold her hand, and occasionally caress her back
2. Thank her for cooking	→ Treat her to a candle light dinner
3. Open the car door for her and pull her chair out for her	→ Tell her how nice she looks
4. Take her on a special vacation of her choice	→ Shower her with gifts and love on her with your words and affection.

Good Hygiene

Most women do not have a problem with good smelling hygiene. It is the nature of a woman to smell good every chance she gets. If it's not the sweet smelling fragrance, it's the red bottom pumps to add. Just had to throw that in there. She wants to make her appearance grand every chance she gets. Women tend to lean to sweet fragrances out on market and run to try them. However, there are some women who struggle in this area especially if they were not raised in this way. Some women had to struggle all of their lives just to make ends meet, and a sweet smelling fragrance is the last thing on their mind. Not to say that she still would not purchase sweet smelling items, it just would not be her first choice. Survival would be in consideration.

In the case of good hygiene, I not only speak of a good smelling fragrance of cologne, but also a good scent without cologne. This also helps just as a scent on an ordinary day, or when preparing for your wife right before making love, during lovemaking, or a heated romance. It is embarrassing when your bad hygiene ruins the moment in every occasion and outing. You would not want your wife to turn the other way and hold her nose or look funny because she knows others are laughing at your negative aroma. Hygiene matters if you want to keep the fire burning in your marriage. It is a complete turn off when hygiene and bad breath keeps your needs from being met because she can't stand to get close to you. You must check that and keep it in check.

Appearance Matter
Most men can be very simple in making choices for dressing nice. It does not take much to put together a nice outfit for him. Women love it when a man looks like a man and act like a man, and vice versa, a man loves it when a woman looks and acts like a woman. They two are not competing. They two are complimenting. So pay close attention to how you smell and look. You do not want to be misjudged or mistaken by looking like a negative of somebody else on the outside, rather than the nice handsome man you are on the inside.

Believe it or not, women do not like a man with dirty nails and crusty feet. Most men laugh at other guys for getting manicures and pedicures. However, there is nothing wrong with this. You can still look strong and have strong looking hands and feet while at the same time having clean nails and feet. No woman wants her spouse's dirty smelly hands and scaly feet all over them nor while trying to be romantic. This is an immediate turn off. And, you can't get mad at her for not allowing you to go further than the initial foreplay because of dirty smelly hands and scaly feet scrapping her legs. Because if the shoe was on the other foot, you wouldn't want it either. It doesn't matter how long you two have been married.

Staying well groomed plays a big part in good hygiene. For example, keeping your hair, mustache and beard (if you have any) cut and groomed on a regular basis; and your clothes ironed and not wrinkled. Women like to show their man off and what a terrible thing when she is turned off because of this imbalance. Her needs are important and they matter in every way.

Verbally Loved

A simple "I love you" on a daily basis tears down stress buildups that may have accumulated on that day for her and you. It is not always a long conversation your wife is looking for, sometimes she's just needing you to say, "I love you and hope you've had a good day." Not a long lecture about the house is dirty and why haven't she started dinner yet, and the dog is all over the place and out of control, the couch smells like pee and that she needs to tend to it. Or, you hungry and that you haven't eaten all day syndrome. Everyone carries their own weight. There is something for each partner to do. There is a responsibility for each partner to do. The wife does not have all of the responsibility and the husband has none. They both has equal share and they both work together. They both win together. One do not go before the other, they both win at the same time. So do not make her feel as if she's working a double shift rather than leaving the job at work and being excited about seeing her husband; and if you two have kids, seeing them too when she gets home.

It is a very stressful thing when she has to come home to nagging and un-appreciativeness. It is terrible for a woman who has worked long hours to have to come home to cook all of her children dinner and a husband that has been home all day, and could have helped her out by either cooking for her and the kids (if any) or buying something for them all to eat. It is a together thing. This is what helps make a marriage last, rather than end up in a horrific divorce; and adding to the statistic of another marriage gone bad whether a Christian marriage or a none Christian marriage. You must learn what works for you two and keep doing that. What works for your marriage may not work for another marriage. But, you do you and allow God to do the rest. It will be a rewarding lasting marriage always. This is why we hear from time to time a seasoned marriage of 50 and 60 years still going strong, because they found what works for them and they regard these things in this book, "Winning Together" as rewarding for them. Taking time to do this will result in a better husband, loving husband, better wife, loving wife, because they will do the same back to the other.

Perfection is always key in any relationship. No one's by far perfect. In fact, the more you try to be perfect, the more you realize that you are not. So, make a list and point out those areas of weakness you have and those areas your spouse is suggesting, and try to work on them. This is what builds relationship and lasting covenant partnership. Abraham and Sarah had a long loving lasting covenant partnership and relationship. It is shown in the Bible that they were not a perfect couple, however, with every imperfection; they strived to better themselves as well as each other. Why? Because they loved each other and they loved God and cared about how He felt about them individually as well as both together. Believe it or not, God cares about all of these things I have mentioned in this book concerning the marriage—you and her—your needs matter—the importance of her needs and that they matter too.

Please understand that you are not her daddy. She does not need an egotistical controlling or an abusive freak. What she needs is a loving, patient, caring, and sensitive to her needs husband; and always making her feel like a beautiful woman and that her needs are important too.

Made to Feel Strong

It is by right that the husband is the head of the household. This is why it is very important for him to make sure that all of his decisions are from a biblical base point of view. They should never come from what you feel is the right thing to do or the right bills to pay at that time, or miss paying your tithes this month or that month, or switching the kids from this school to that school just because they do not like a certain teacher, or making a negative choice on purpose because you know your wife is right and you do not want her to control you. This is not the kind of made to feel strong I am talking about. The made to feel strong I am talking about is, although you are the head of the household, it is nothing wrong with allowing your wife to have a say so in the matter and be right and you two **AGREE** to go with what she suggested. Do not make her feel like a slave and being controlled by her master. Those are the ol' days and God's Will, will never be done. You two are <u>ONE</u> and she needs to feel important too and not feel like a child.

If your wife is not where she needs to be in terms of being the wife that she needs to be to you and if you two have kids, to them as well, do not make her feel as if she will never get to that delivered place. Build her up by telling her how much you appreciate her trying and to keep trying and that she's doing a great job. This builds faith, pushes, and motivates her to get better; rather to get negative and judgmental let downs that tear her down and then she's worse off than she's ever been before. She already has enough on her to see about her wife duties and mother duties (if this applies), and she needs your help to be positive and keep her lifted up, not torn down. If this is a no win for you as a husband, stay quiet, pray and allow God to help her get where she needs to be until you see a way to get inside and encourage.

I realize there are some men who disagree with making a woman feel strong. However, if you think about it, who would want a weak woman or wife? I've been around plenty of men and not one have stated that they like a weak woman. All those who did, they are no longer in that relationship. They get bored and say that she's not a challenge and always do what he tells her to do. All she wants to do is hang under him and never have a balance, and go hang with friends as well. Too clingy and so on.

As I have stated in the chapter for her, both of you cannot be strong and aggressive together at the same time. There is a balance and there is a season. What I mean by this is, there are times when a woman gets weak and needs her husband to step up and be strong until she can get herself together. For example, she may have lost her job and need you to pay bills until she can find a new job. This is what I mean by one being strong while the other is submitted until things get back in order. You two are working together and not competing for control, and taking revenge when it appears that you are no longer in control and make things worse. This can result in a dysfunctional marriage and could possibly lead to divorce.

I have counseled with women and they all have almost said the same thing, "he doesn't make me feel like a woman", or "he's always putting me down like I'm the only one wrong", or "He never admits his faults", or "he doesn't listen to me", or "his way or no way", or "He never shuts up", or "he won't let the past go", or "He's always calling me fat", or "He comes in all kinds of late hours, I know he's sleeping around." These are some common jesters but they are jesters that need to take notice if you are a husband and want to better your marriage. It should be your goal to win in marriage not to give up and become lazy and defeated. Marriage should be something beautiful between a man and woman, not grievous.

Her Needs Are Important

It is a competitive thing with men not to let the "girl" beat them. This type of competition mechanism is a generational stereo type that most men have been raised with. The word "competitor" has no name or gender on it. In terms of the marriage, it should not have no place. If you as a husband have a problem with your spouse being the breadwinner, you should evaluate why you got married in the first place. This type of behavior can hinder and break your marriage a part. It is important to get everything out in the open before you two get married so that if there is any disagreement, you two can either come together, pray about it, consider feelings, and try to work them out, or you two have the chance to go your separate ways. That is a must rather than get married without being completely honest, allow the stress of the unspoken truth escalate, and blows up years later. The divorce rate is higher than it has ever been, even in the Christian marriage. You must realize that you are not the only one who will be detrimentally affected, but many others will as well—family, kids (if any), friends, job, custody battles, financial settlements—who gets what, shares—401k plans, etc.

Taunting her about how she looks or how heavy she is out of the question. It only makes matters worse. You as her husband should never make fun of your wife. You chose to be with her and you must have seen something beautiful then. So with the same feeling and love you had when you first met her, is the same feeling and love you have to have now as you may be years in it with her. As we get older, or bodies change, especially for a woman who have had children, medical issues, or heavy weight runs in her family. It can be a challenge. However, you made the choice to be with her and therefore, you should love her just as if you had the same struggle or worse. You may encourage her as you two can get fitness memberships together, run and train together, and make a strict eating plan/diet for you both. These always help and is never wrong.

How to Spark Her Flames

Women love to be loved. A woman loves for a man to rub and touch her when she is in love, and vice versa. This is simply the result of the love connection that is between the two. The man gives, the woman receives. But in turn, a woman can also give too. Your goal as a man should be to take care of her sexually, passionately, affectionately, verbally, mentally, emotionally, and spiritually *(reading your Bible together, going to church together, praying, fasting, and worshiping together, etc.)*. It is not about you getting pleased at that moment. It is all about pleasing her and making sure she is well satisfied. This sparks her flames. In this case, you as the man should pay close attention to her every movement and study what pleases her and what does not. There again, it is not about you at this moment, it is about her totally. Her needs are most important.

Each couple is different. Therefore, the needs are different. What works for one couple, may not work for the other one. So, this is why I made the point to watch your mate very close and see what pleases her and what does not, and make every effort to please her in every way. Pleasing her is not always sexually, in fact, it may just be conversationally, emotionally, affectionately, romantically, comically, just relaxing together with nothing said, or just enjoying one another's presence. There are times when a man can act unconcerned outside, but on the inside he may be very concerned but do not know how to show it. You can ruin the mood by doing this because she can only see what you are putting out rather than what is really going on on the inside of you. So, I say to you it is okay to show your feelings and emotions. You are not considered soft if you do. Your spouse knows you and she wants, yearns, and needs this from you when that time arises. This helps bring greater passionate love, better understanding emotionally and conversationally, which builds a lasting partnership.

I encourage you as the man to hold your wife and allow her to rest in your arms. Know what to say and what not to say at a particular time. Mentioning stressful subjects can quickly change the mood to something drastic and detrimental. It is okay to hold her and rest. Believe me, she is holding you and resting in your arms her own way. And, with this, you can still feel strong and feel a sense of protecting her. Take advantage of the moment, your biggest release will come.

Just as I stated in the last chapter that a woman cannot change a man, well, a man cannot change a woman. It is important for you as a man to let a woman be a woman. Stop trying to change everything about her. The way she walk, the way she dress, the way she talk, who she hang with, why she bath that way, or why she put her shirt on before putting her pants on first. This is non-sense. Just let her do her. Another one is, if she just lost her job, don't ride her about bills, and who's going to get the kids from school, and go on a cursing rampage. Do not keep reminding her about her being unemployed and all she wants to do is watch the stories all day, eat, and get fat. You never know you may fall in the same situation she's in and will need her strength, encouragement, love, and spiritual support.

If loving your wife is hard because of hurt or unhappiness, it wasn't what you expected, she doesn't turn you on, is not romantic, or is abusive, etc., you need to seek help right away. It is good to first talk with your spouse and then you two make the decision from there. I have seen cases where the wife was a wonderful, perfect woman and the man just could not love her the way she wanted him to love her and needed to be loved. He was dealing with past issues in which stopped him from being affectionate and able to please her enough. As a result, the relationship eventually deteriorated with the worst shocking case of infidelity.

As I stated earlier, generational curses from the parent on down the bloodline will have an effect on your marriage if you do not pray and seek God for deliverance. For example, if the husband has come from a molested, rejected, abusive home, he may be withdrawn from the wife. As a result, he may not have a desire to kiss you when you get home or before bedtime. He may not have a desire to make love or when you want it. He may push you away when you're trying to turn him on physically. He may yell at you when you buy him a watch as opposed to new shoes—never satisfied. He may even yell and lash out at you for no reason. He may even not say a word. Squeezing a word out of him is like squeezing an over ripped lemon.

One thing that disturbs me to see is hateful men with loving good women. And vice versa, a hateful woman with a loving good man. They always say, good women are hard to find and good men are hard to find. Can you literally ask yourself "Am I a good man or a hateful man? Which one would you answer to? Why? Answer below:

_____
_____
_____
_____
_____

Communication is the Key to Every Winning Together Relationship. It is the key when it is shared truthfully. No matter what is shared. An example is listed below:

> **_From the Female Point of View:_** "I hate it when you fart loud all the time, or when your feet stink up the house and you do not clean them, but I do like it when you rub my back and tell me you love me."
>
> **_From the Male Point of View:_** "I hate it when you don't fix your hair and you pull your wig off when we're cuddling, keep the house dirty, or be too possessive, but I like it when you rub my back and support me in my decisions."

If you two want to win, there must be truthful communication and respect to make changes to areas your spouse is not happy with. You are the bigger one when you can admit when you're wrong, and strive to win by perfecting those areas of struggle until they are gone.

Respect Her Woman Cave:
A woman cave is a place just for women. It is a woman's desire and inspiration to design a space just for her. It is where a woman can go get some peace away from her husband, kids (if any), and anybody else. It is also known as, a lady cave or a mom cave. Some unhappy women would agree that any name will do to keep out pestering kids and a nagging husband. While other happy women would address it as a safe-haven, a temporary time alone from the kids and husband, but yet, once her time is spent, she returns to her happy husband and kids.

Every woman just like a man with a man cave needs her space. I hope that I explained this well in the last chapter, just the other way around. Getting with the girls often don't hurt. It allows her to some time to vent about women stuff and pamper herself without having to share herself. The expectations and obligations of a wife and or a mother is great. It can become overwhelming if she allows it to. Her woman cave is not always filled with a bunch of women, gossiping social gatherings, manicures, pedicures, and massage parties. At times, if not most times, it is a place where she can be alone away from everything and everybody.

You as her partner must understand that if there is a need and it is not a drastic need, respect her by leaving her alone until she comes out. For example, if there are no clean new towels to dry your hands off on but the one you've been using, just use the one you have until the next day instead of looking to her to wash new ones at 11 o'clock at night. You as her partner must respect her time if you want your marriage or relationship to continue to be strong and keep the love flowing. It is something about time away that brings release, recuperation, and equal partnership.

A woman cave may be located in different places:
1. A bathroom *(enjoying soaking in the bath tub)*
2. A walk-in closet
3. A basement
4. A garage
5. A guest room or room other than the master bedroom you and him share
6. Covered patio *(preferably in the back yard)*
7. *A tree house*
8. *The guest house*

The woman cave may have a little more places to hide out than the man. Most men, not all, don't soak in a tub everyday and you wouldn't find very many relaxing in a closet. However, women will go wherever there is peace, quiet, and comfort. Wherever her cave is, you should respect that and be patient as you give her, her space and time to recuperate.

I have provided some scenarios in which men say toward their wives having a woman cave. This scenario is not one that the two agreed on:

Scenario 1:

My wife didn't think about having this so-called woman cave until she heard one of her female friends talking about it. She's turned into this cave freak with pink everywhere, decorative fabric all on the walls and couches, candles lit up. A bit too much for me. She's always in her hide out with nothing done here in the real life world house. I wish she would spend more time cooking and cleaning doing the duties she's supposed to do as a wife. She took the basement and turned it into this fancy world. I hate it and do not agree with it.

This next scenario is more of an understanding one:

Scenario 2:

I love when my wife goes to her woman cave. It gives me a chance to go to my man cave. And, when I want some company over to watch the football or basketball games with in my man cave, I feel comfortable because I know she agrees with it. We both respect each other's time away and as a result, it has made our relationship stronger and more fun when we come together and go out and spend quality time together.

This last scenario is one that may seem off the wall, but is true in most homes but most will not admit it:

Scenario 3:

My woman cave went soar when some of the ladies invited some of their lady friends over and brought drinks and things got out of hand. We were so loud and disruptive that my husband came in the room and put all of the women out and he and I got into it. Since then we separated. I have not seen or heard from him in about a week. Lucky we do not have any kids or else I would file a missing report. Maybe I shouldn't have had my girls over and been so loud? But I still believe there is nothing wrong with having a little fun. He should've stayed in his place.

In situations like these, it is vital to communicate truthfully and come to an agreement with your spouse especially on subjects like these just stated. It can have its negative feedback as well as rewards if you two communicate instead of looking at it in a selfish way as if your opinion only matters.

Below are some questions you and your partner or a group can talk about concerning having a woman cave:

Do you think the husband should be allowed in the wife's woman cave? Why? Why not?

Why do you need a woman cave?

Should you and your husband have a woman cave together? Why? Why not?

Her Needs Are Important

Should the man control how the woman cave looks? Why? Why not?

Should your husband control <u>who to</u> invite to your woman cave? Why? Why not?

Should your husband control <u>who you</u> invite to your woman cave? Why? Why not?

Should the kids hang out in the woman cave? Why? Why not?

What are your thoughts on each scenario? State them below for personal use and for group discussion.

CHAPTER 9
If You Want the Pink Panties, You Got to Buy the Pink Panties

f you want pink panties, you got to buy pink panties. If you want red bottom pumps, you got to buy red bottom pumps. If you want the fitted dress suit, you got to buy the fitted dress suit. Many times, women and men want things from their spouses and from the relationship but are not willing to put their best into getting it for them. No, you cannot change a person, but you can love them and suggest enhancements. It is called, give a little take a little. Both parties should win in this area. No one is left out because you both are getting what you want. You make a suggestion and she makes a suggestion. Both needs are met. Neither of you should feel uncomfortable because as the Bible says, the *"bed is undefiled"* (Hebrews 13:4). Meaning, there is nothing that is defiled about making love with your spouse and the spontaneous things or ways you use to make it a memorable lasting moment. There is nothing wrong with wanting to see your spouse in a nice fitted dress suit. There is nothing wrong with spicing it up a little. No one wants to become old, wrinkled up and run down with one another. Excitement helps the heart grow fonder. Get it? Good.

While the look helps draw in the mood in your private space, it is understood that men do not want to see their spouse in large panties that hide their shape all the time. There are times when a man wants his wife in something that will make him say, "Babe, you are so sexy". Not you wearing something that will make him turn his face and laugh or become very angry. As you both are around other couples, you do not want your spouse to throw out embarrassing hinting words of, "see what so and so is wearing? Now I can dig that. Why don't you dress like that?" You want his attention totally on you saying, "Honey, I really like what you are wearing. You look really nice."

Getting mad at the same ol' things is a waste of time. They are repetitive, redundant, and childish. It is a waste of time to get mad because she is not romantic the way you want her to be, or she is not at all. You may have to take the first step to help her to please you by showing her what you want and what you like and how you like it. She cannot read your mind. And, if she has never had a romantic marriage, it will take a minute to get her there. As I stated before, it may take you taking charge and taking her to the store and showing her exactly what you like; as you go without fussing or making negative smart remarks about the way she looks or what you are not pleased with. It should be peaceful and fun, and not nasty and grievous. Think of it this way, your spouse would never do anything to hurt you and you like wise. So bring it all together and make it happen.

Scenario 1:

Ramona just got home from a day's work as Jim, her husband, did to. They two prepare to unwind for bed as Jim took is bath first and now Ramona is in and out right behind him. Jim secretly has an issue with Ramona not dressing romantically when they get in the bed every night. It does not help the fact that his buddies on his job brags about their wives wearing sexy velvet and satin panties and pajamas to bed—they know how to set the romantic mood.

He does not want to hurt Ramona's feelings so he puts up with her huge panties and 2x t-shirt. Jim has a fetish for big shirts and huge old fashion panties. The more he went to work, the more his buddies and co-workers bragged on their wives. It came to a place where he did not want to go around them anymore because he was too embarrassed and it made him very depressed. It wasn't that he wanted Ramona to wear sexy panties and lingerie's to bed every night, but he wanted to feel like she was his wife and not some sleeping partner with no attraction.

One day Jim unexpectedly met up with one of his longtime friends he hadn't seen in years at a local convenient store while pumping gas. They got in a conversation about their wives and somehow what was bothering Jim came out to the open. Come to find out, his friend dealt with the same thing with his wife years ago. He suggested that Jim go to the store and surprise his wife with Victoria's Secret satin panties and lingerie, and some Bath and Body Works bath soap. Jim mentioned to his friend that she was very sensitive and that would not be a good idea. So his friend suggested that he take her and they both get something together. Jim immediately took him up on what he suggested and left with his phone number and a new determination to win in this area that he was not pleased with.

As soon as he got home, Ramona had beat him there as always. He mentioned to her about going shopping on the weekend. Ramona surprisingly agreed and they set out that weekend.

Jim took her to other stores before going to Victoria's Secret to throw off what he really wanted from Ramona. It worked. They finally arrived in the store and to Jim's surprise, Ramona burst in tears and said, "this is what I have always been wanting from you. I just didn't know how to tell you." The fact that Ramona did not grow up like that did not help with pleasing him. Jim shed a tear and they both found themselves two sexy sets of lingerie and matching pajamas. Ramona has sexy pink panties with a matching spaghetti strap top, and Jim has satin green trunks with a satin button down shirt to match he found at a men's store nearby. They then set off to Bath and Body Works and found some smell goods—one for her and one for him.

That night was a night to remember as Ramona and Jim came out of the bathroom together, looking and smelling stunning.

Every night from that day forward Ramona and Jim has made it their priority to go shopping for new things every weekend to add to their bedtime wardrobe. Old flames were finally rekindled.

The question is, why did it take Jim doing something special for Ramona to come out and tell the truth? Why wasn't Jim upfront with Ramona considering they are married partners and should be able to talk about anything that is bothering them? What do you think was Ramona's upbringing that may have caused her not to wear sexy pajamas that pleased her husband? Should Jim have handled this situation another way? Should he have shared his business with a friend he had not seen in years instead of talking his personal business with his wife? Was Jim's friend God sent? Did Ramona and Jim both become too relaxed considering they were not newlyweds anymore and the kinky and sexiness was not necessary anymore? How would you have handled this if this were you in this same position, either as Ramona or Jim, or as both? Why? And how? Write your answers below and if you are in a group, talk about it with them.

If You Want the Pink Panties, You Got to Buy the Pink Panties

CHAPTER 10
If You Want the Briefs,
You Got to Buy
the Briefs.

When you think of the title above, the first thought that might come to your mind may be something perverted or kinky. Well, it is not to be taken as such. As I have stated in the last chapter, as I geared it toward the wife and now toward to husband, "the bed is undefiled" (Hebrews 13:4). What this means is that it is not perverted to wear briefs to bed with your wife.

If you want the briefs, you got to buy the briefs. What this means is, if you as the wife want your husband to look sexy or pleasing to you rather than seeing him in some long, huge ol' fashion and out dated baggy trunks with holes in them, you have got to go the extra mile, as you two come together and go and get the look you want from him. He may not be aware that you are not attracted to that look, or you may not be pleased with it. This mainly happens with more seasoned marriages. Not all, but some. The fact that you two have been married for a long period of time, looking sexy for bed is nowhere in your thoughts and out of the question. Sleep is the only thing on your minds. Again, there is nothing wrong with adding a little spice sometimes. This helps with rekindling the fire in your relationship. You may say our fire is already kindled. And I will say, good but it can get even hotter. You can never stop having fun and enjoying one another. Surely I am not gearing this statement toward sex all the time. I am gearing it toward you wanting him to look nice and be esthetically pleasing to you. His mind is on nothing but pleasing you and you pleasing him.

If you want a tailored suit and tie, go and buy a tailored suit and tie. Many times women fuss about things that they can help their husband change. Although no one can change anybody, there is nothing wrong with a little enhancement for your spouse. If he is always wearing slacks, a button down denim shirt with a long crazy, fruity looking thin tie, you might suggest taking him out to buy a new suit and a new updated tie. It is about communication. You communicate with him and let him know what you like. Most men are simple and it does not take much to please them, while women on the other hand are more elaborate in detail. Both of you should want to please each other. There is something in you that you can upgrade, as well as in him. Work together and come to an agreement. If he does not want to comply, hopefully he will meet you half way. I don't think he will object when it comes to the bedroom, most men don't.

Scenario 1:

Patty and Billy have been married for well over fifteen years. Billy has never been a man of a fine wardrobe. He and Patty met at their Singles Ministry at their church. They hit it off almost immediately and were married soon afterwards.

Patty always throws hints to Billy about the way he dresses, which was and is the only turn off she has about him. Most would ask why did she marry him considering the pet peeve of the way he dresses was and still is so depressing to her. She mentioned to them that she got in it because she knew he was a good Godly man, she loved how he made her feel, and for other unethical reasons she had to admit.

Billy's main wardrobe is blue jeans and t-shirt. He even wears the same black slacks and a white or a long sleeve emerald blue button down shirt with a tie to match. The church members stare at him every Sunday, which makes Patty sink in her seat. She did not have the nerve to talk to Billy about the way he dresses because he comes off as being an overly aggressive man. She is very intimidated of him.

Billy's birthday was around the corner and Patty wondered what to buy him. Her thought quickly came to a new suit, tie, and some gator shoes.

She bought just what her thoughts suggested.

On Billy's birthday, Patty didn't know Billy would react the way he did. She thought he would be very upset with her. However, Billy was more simple minded than she thought. He was very easy going and excited. She quickly found out that the suit, tie, and gator shoes were what he had prayed for. She was ecstatic and suggested that he dress like that to church and everywhere from that day forward. He immediately agreed and asked about going to buy more suits and updated clothing. He couldn't believe how good he looked.

When they went to church, everybody gave so many compliments. Some gave them with tears in their eyes as they all couldn't keep their eyes off Billy. He needed that boost from Patty to pull out the best in him.

The question is, why didn't Patty just talk to her husband about how she was embarrassed with his out dated wardrobe? Why was she intimidated considering that was her husband and she should feel comfortable? Why did it take fifteen years for Patty to help her husband? Why did Patty hold her embarrassment and depression for fifteen years before opening up and being honest with Billy? Can you imagine what the new

Billy looks like? How would you have handled this if this were you in this same position, either as Patty or Billy, or as both? Why? And how? Write your answers below and if you are in a group, talk about it with them.

11
CHAPTER
Romantic Love Rekindles the Fire and Keeps it Burning

Candle lights are the norm when it comes to sparking the romantic mood. If the question is asked, "how do I set the mood for me and my spouse?" The answer is always the norm, set up a candle light dinner. It's funny because although it is the norm, it works every time. The mood is immediately set especially if the environment is set just right. That is the purpose, you want the smell and the environment to be just right because anything out of order just a little bit can spoil the mood and the night altogether. God could not have created a more powerful thing called, "romance". Romance is a part of love. God gave us love as He exemplified it Himself. The bed is undefiled. The married couple is welcomed to do what pleases them both. Without romance, there is no possible way the fire can kindle or be rekindled. For example, I counseled a couple who all they did was get into it with each other. So I thought of recommending that they both do something nice and romantic for one another all week until we all met again. They argued at the suggestion at first, but after they went to the store and got in the mood, their attitudes quickly changed to an immediate turn around, and did something romantic as it rekindled the fire between them. The husband sent her flowers to her job everyday of the week. And she sent cards to his job and placed special love notes around the house for him to read.

The breakthrough was them getting out and having a picnic in the park and going to buy romantic outfits. Sometimes you have to change your environment that will get you in the mood for change. For example, before they went out to the store to look for romantic things, they had no feeling of romance (in the office). But once they went to the park and got out to the store and saw all the romantic outfits and smell goods, their attitudes and moods quickly changed. The fire began to burn for each other just that quick. They forgot about everything that bothered them about each other. They ended up spending more money than they thought they would and made plans to go back to the store.

Romance comes in many ways, however, you two have to do whatever is romantic for your two and make it work. If it is just sitting on the couch in each other's arms, eating popcorn, watching a movie, or breakfast in bed, rekindle your fire that way. If it is eating dinner together, rekindle your fire that way. If it is taking a bath or shower together, rekindle your fire that way. Whatever works for you two to keep the fire burning, do it. No one can keep the fire burning between you two but you two. No one can be right where you are and coach you in detail on how to do it, but you two. Go with what you feel as you have received some ideas in this book and make it work for you two.

Scenario 1:

Reba and Jesse Lee loves old westerns. They watch them almost every chance they get. The fact that they live way out in the deep woods of the country gives them no room to go shopping or to the movies regularly. Jesse Lee always likes to do romantic things for Reba as he is very affectionate and romantic. He does almost everything a person can do in the country for romance: have romantic sex in the woods, pick sweet smelling flowers from the woods and surprise her with them, ride horses together, swim in a lake together, hunt together, ride the tracker to a romantic place in the country area and have picnics, him chauffeuring her with a boat ride down the lake, and so on. This time Reba suggested they just sit in front of the TV and watch an old western and rekindle the fire that way. Jesse Lee made no objections and quickly agreed. Their love was rekindled again that night together.

The question is, was the way Reba and Jesse Lee rekindled their fire too simple? Should they have been more creative? Why didn't they do something in the woods instead of watching TV? Why did they have sex in the woods as a married couple, do you think that was appropriate? Do you think all of his romantic spontaneity was good ones? How would you have rekindled the fire if this were you in this same position, either as Reba or Jesse Lee, or as both? Why? And how? Write your answers below and if you are in a group, talk about it with them.

12

CHAPTER

Relationship Builder:
*Knowing What Turns
Him on & Finding Out
What Affection She
Likes*

What builds a relationship? Building a relationship takes teamwork. It takes coming together and working as one—a bonding partnership. It is one in which holds no secrets. Forgives easily with no grudges and hidden agendas. There are too many couples and marriages that hold secrets and yet appear to be as one. It does not work like that. You must not hold anything back if you want to be as one. Spirituality must be the center of the relationship. There must be a balance and spirituality should be at the top of the list. Spirituality is what gets you two to the Father (God). He is the only One that can and will give you two the wisdom and the direction you both need when making choices and decisions.

Knowing What Turns Him On:

It is important to know what turns him on. I have mentioned this all through my book. This is the center of attention in every relationship. I'm sure it is not one of the first that every person looks for, but it is certainly not far from the top of the list. If you cannot turn him on, it becomes a problem. He gets bored and looks elsewhere to who can. It is sad to admit, but it is the same in every case whereas he is not getting what he needs is always the words. Or, if she would give him more time, he can deal with some of the negatives she has.

Sex is not always the center of conversation when it comes to pleasing him. Although there are some men that want to be pleased in this way, it is not always that way with every man. And, every man does not want you to please them in a strip club, but he would like a satisfying conversation or hearing something he likes. This can turn him on. You are pleasing him in conversation, letting him know how special he is, how strong and loving he is. You are building up his inner horizons, which tantalizes his needs and makes him want to turn and please you. I will give an example of a conversation: maybe talk about a good football game or basketball game. It may be stupid, better yet boring to you but it turns him on just to know that you care about the things he likes and the fact that you care enough to try and make him happy.

A simple kiss after a long day at work or out and about will also add to turning him on. Many women miss this. They are so wrapped up in taking care of the needs of the house and or even getting the kids straight that they miss pleasing him. There are also some who are selfish and want him to make the first move all of the time, rather than make the first move themselves. These little things matter. I talk more about these areas in the chapters, *"His Needs Matter"*, *"Her Needs Are Important."*

Finding Out What Affection She Likes:
Finding out what affection she likes. It is a waste of time to be in a relationship and not want to know what turns your partner on. Pleasing her should be your number one agenda. Of course, 24-7 would be a bit too much and overwhelming, however, you can come as close to it as possible, especially if it keeps her and you satisfied.

Sex or hanging out in a strip club is not always the satisfaction that a woman is looking for. Most to all times it is not, especially for a Christian marriage (concerning hanging out in a strip club). This also is the same for a man. There are many other things that can be done to please her that is much better than sex being number one on your agenda. For example, a walk in the park while holding hands without sex being the subject of conversation. Another example is, having a good conversation on the subject that she likes. I have encountered men who only want to talk about themselves or what matters only to them. He never gives any attention to what she likes, if caring for that matter. They are so wrapped up in themselves that they never let her have a word in edge wise. This is a major turn off for a woman or spouse. A woman wants a man that is not always about himself but can share in the conversation and make himself the lesser in order to please her at that moment. This is a turn on for a woman. When she can express herself and feel free to talk about what she likes, you have won her attention and happiness.

You may ask how can you please her in conversation? What can you talk about? You should first study her and find out what she likes. Actually, this should have been done the moment you two met. However, since it wasn't, you can now watch her and ask her what she likes. Just as I shared above about how the woman can please the man by asking and talking about football and/or basketball, well, it works the same for the woman. If she sows clothing, you can talk about that. If she likes reading, you can ask her what book is she reading and what is it about. You can also talk about sports too. They may or may not like football or basketball, but they like volleyball, cheerleading, or track and field. It is about watching and finding out what pleases her and what turns her on. If you do not watch or act concern, you miss out on pleasing her and she will become bored and distant with you. Again, it is not always about sex. If she is a good woman, sex may not be in the conversation at first or at all, but these other conversations will. If you have been with her for a long period of time, sex may be the last thing on her mind to turn her on, but these other areas will spark her up again. You never want a woman to think that all you want is sex and nothing else. This will always be a turn off, but when you look at all the other areas who make her who she is: the beautiful, loving, God-fearing woman that she is will always turn her on.

You may say, "it is too expensive to please her. My money is always short or I may not make as much as she does." She may be the breadwinner in your relationship. I will tell you that it does not always take money to turn her on. It is, at most times, the little things that I have mentioned above that turn her on. And, they are free. Spark conversations about what she likes, walks in the park, romantic walks along the local lake, beach, or neighborhood, a car ride around town as you two enjoy one another's company (without the kid(s) (if any); and also you can take naps together and just hold one another without making love.

Pride will stop you from pleasing her. Unforgiveness will stop you from pleasing her as well. Scars from your childhood and past (marriages, relationships, job, church, etc.) will stop you from pleasing her. Abuse will stop you from pleasing her as well. If you are hitting on her or abusing her verbally will stop you from pleasing her. If these areas are not dealt with, they will stop you from having a wholesome, loving relationship that you always longed for from a woman. They will also stop you from pleasing her in every way possible. These are the areas that satan works keenly in—abuse on all levels: physical, verbal, emotional- making her feel that she's always doing something wrong when she is right, striking up arguments just to upset her and for the heck of it. If satan can destroy the marriage, he can destroy the family. And if he can destroy the family, he can destroy everything.

You may ask, how do I deal with these hidden scars and issues so that I can please my partner and be happy? I will answer:

1. You first must admit that you have a problem to God, to yourself, then to him or her (repent for your wrong).

2. You then must deal with these issues by talking to each other. Make sure you share everything you need in order to get totally free. Get everything out, keeping nothing hidden.

3. Then you must deal with these issues through prayer. You two should openly pray about them together until you release them from within. You may find that as you two begin to pray, you both may have issues or hidden scars that you two need to release. How do you know when you have released them? You release them by crying out, weeping, verbally confessing them, constantly talking through it—not babying the issue, fussing and cursing, or keeping a pity party, but constantly talking it out. You may say, "my partner may not want me to do all of that". I will say, if they love you, they will. I will also say that I'm sure this is what they have been waiting on. I'm sure they have prayed and prayed and finally they can see the manifestation of their prayers come to past. I will tell you another Person Who wants to see you free. His Name is Jesus Christ. He loves you very much and want to see you free if no one else does. He wants you and your spouse to work it out, to get along, have an honest relationship, and live a wholesome loving life together free from drama.

4. You two should go and talk to a counselor or someone you two can trust together who is strong spiritually and can help you two. Sometimes even going to someone that you two do not know can work even better. Sometimes the familiar person may take sides or may be afraid to tell you both the truth. I am not stating that you two should not go to someone you two know and are familiar with, I am stating that it may be better to go to someone you two do not know. However, if you two agree and feel the same way about who to go to, prayed about it, whether you two know them or not, then move on what you two have. It is important to agree at a sensitive and important time as this. Agreement is key. You want to make sure the counselor or listener is God sent and is chosen and is going to help and benefit your relationship; and help you get free or else it will be a waste of time. You are not meeting with them for a social gathering. This is why I mentioned about going to someone you do not know. However, if you all have an understanding, it is fine. It is not a male or female thing, it is a whoever is chosen to successfully help you two thing. Pray about it, God will surely show you who. And when He does, please do not reject him or her because they are not who you want or think that they can help you (physical appearance, male or female, etc.) because you may miss out on a blessing and a complete change you and your spouse have prayed about.

5. Once these points are complete, you will then want to leave it alone. Once you have gotten it all out, and feel and know that you are completely free, you can now move on with your relationship and life together. There is nothing like the feeling of freedom, to be free from something or some things you have been holding and bound for years, let alone for decades, is one of the greatest feelings in the world.

Scenario 1:

It was a sad day for Greeny. He have just lost his job with chances of being unemployed for a while. He and his wife Kim was having a romantic moment and all of a sudden Greeny raises his voice and asks, "I'm mad because you are late paying the cable and light bill?" Greeny completely threw everything off and spoiled the romantic mood, which made Kim sit up in the bed with tears in her eyes as she pressed her hands in her face. She knew Greeny was taking his frustrations out on her and she did not appreciate it. He never asked her did she pay the two bills, he assumed that she just didn't pay them and was mad about it.

Come to find out, Kim did pay the bills and had not yet shown him the receipts.

The question is, why would Greeny take his frustrations out on Kim? Why would he spoil the romantic mood for something so childish as a bill

Relationship Builder

payment? Was Greeny really taking his frustrations out on Kim, or was he a mean person regardless? Why didn't Kim confront him with the truth when she sat up in the bed? Was effective communication the key here? Was effective relationship building the key here? How would you have handled the moment if this were you in this same position, either as Kim or Greeny, or as both? Why? And how? Write your answers below and if you are in a group, talk about it with them.

Relationship Builder

CHAPTER 13
Fruit & Toys
Are Undefiled

It is said in Hebrews 13:4 that the marriage is honorable and the bed is undefiled. I realize the phrase; "Fruit & Toys Are Undefiled" may sound to some to be unpurified and to others somewhat kinky. My thing is, pick what side you're on. I find it always safe to follow what the Word of God says when it comes to what a married couple can do in the bedroom, especially as a Christian couple.

One night I was watching a Christian channel and a Christian couple was on there speaking about their marriage and one of them said, "when we first got married, I was confused as to what song to make love to." Everyone laughed including the audience. Then he said, "But when I came across the scripture in Hebrews where it talks about the bed being undefiled, it gave me peace as to what song to make my partner and I more comfortable to make love and be at peace with it. The preacher who was interviewing them blurts in with a laugh and says, "I realize it's hard to make love to your spouse to "Jesus is on the main line, tell em' what you want..." Everyone really laughed at that and so did I. Just the sound and music of the song brought an uninviting mood change to my imagination just thinking about it. Don't get me wrong, it was not the Name Jesus and the ministry of the song, it was the Spirit of it. That song brings praise and worship. When you think of making love to your spouse, you think of something romantic to set the mood. Those two have no similarity.

The key word to remember is, "undefiled". Meaning, there is nothing impure about what you do with your partner in the bed or behind closed doors. In fact, it brings more pleasure and spontaneity to what you two as you two can invite more exciting ideas and exercises to your private place. I have found as I have counseled married couples in the past that it sparks the fire and keeps it burning. I encourage you to back track and concentrate on the previous chapter, chapter eleven, "Romantic Love Rekindles the Fire and Keeps it Burning" if you need help in this area or want to further your questioned mind, this chapter will do that for you.

Toys come in all shapes, sizes, colors, and names. However, the toys I am speaking of are toys that turns you and your partner on. You can take your pick on what type of toy. I am not encouraging you to add evil or devilish items, or toys that will invite evil into your romantic place and spoil the mood. I am saying keep it clean and simple. Get together and

Fruit & Toys Are Undefiled

find a special toy that fits you and her or him, and go with that. For example, using a radio with the right music is one. Choosing the right music is so important. It can either set the mood or break the mood of great, passionate intimacy. It can either unite passionate love, or destroy passionate love. Massaging toys (electrical or non-electrical) are also good, especially after a long stressful day. You can slowly massage your partner's back or body with lotion or baby oil to make the massage more pleasing and relaxing. This brings great foreplay (sexual activity that precedes sexual intercourse). Lotion is another toy. You can use this item to massage with great pleasure on your spouse. The kind that has an awesome fragrance is always the best ones for both partners. Whatever brings you and your partner intimate, passionate love that pleases you both is what you go with.

Passionate love means to give it all you got. It's funny because you may sweat on this one. If passionate love is forced without connection, it will drive you and your spouse to sweat with an unnecessary workout. I'm sure you get the picture. My thing is, just enjoy your covenant sex partner and not be grieved because they are not exciting or not enough. To each their own, but make sure husband's you are her hunk for the night, and wife's you are his Victoria's Secret model for the night.

God said in His Word to be "fruitful and multiply". This means, to make passionate love with your spouse, transfer your seed to one another, and multiply with some little I's and mini me's. God encouraged this from the beginning of time when He created Adam and Eve, and told them to be fruitful and to multiply in Genesis 1:22. That was one of God's missions for creating man, to give him a partner to be pleased and to please her; and to multiply—from husband to wife, to a fulfilled family. God loves it when it is done right. This is when we can say that it is undefiled love.

Fruit is always a pleasurable add on when it comes to being spontaneous with your partner in bed or in your private sector. For example, lying in bed while feeding each other chocolate covered strawberries as you dip them in whip cream for more pleasure. Another one is, the honey or fruit massage with your mouth to their body. Stimulates your partner's horizons and gets the fire blazing even more. There are many other ideas that you and spouse can do. You have to use your creative mind and present it to your partner. No one ever writes REAL books like this for the married couple, but this is much needed if you want to keep the fire burning and keep out other unwanted partners.

Marriages can only win if each partner puts forth a 200% effort to be romantic and creative in the bed and in their relationship. No one is there to judge but you, your spouse, and God. If these things make you and your spouse uncomfortable, then try something else. If these things make you both comfortable, then keep doing it as long as it continues to work. You can never go wrong doing things that make you two happy and it builds intimacy and keeps your marriage romantic, spontaneous, strong, and as one. I only recommend this for the married couple. Any other would be defiled, impure, and sinful to God.

Somehow, I can hear a couple asking, "We would love to try this, but how can we do this with our children or our family in the house?" My answer to you would be to take a <u>you and him</u> night away from the kids and family and go to a hotel, or on a cruise; or even to a close friend or family member's house. You should pre-plan for the night while making preparations to use my examples in my book. From there, allow your romantic horizons to take you wherever you two want to go. There are ways around the cluttered surroundings and kids who always need attention. It is okay to take a break from them and enjoy you and him or her. If you do not, the marriage can become boring and dull.

Below are some examples of what some couples are saying when it becomes dull. I have heard couples say:

- "We do the same ol' things, it's boring and I'm tired and ready to try new things but he or she don't listen."
- "She's always tired and don't wanna' be touched when I'm ready."
- "He always want it one way and never try other ways like I like it."
- "She don't use the sweet smelling soap I like and that is a turn off."
- "His feet stinks and they scratch my legs in bed."
- "She's way too loud, I think she be fakin'."
- Get this one, "He don't like music while making love so it sounds like we're in a cave, and I get embarrassed because I know the whole house can hear us."
- "We tried the massage thing but he's way too rough."
- "We're an old married couple; we're too old for all that stuff."

- "He doesn't foreplay; he just goes right into it, which spoils the mood."
- "She always farts which turns me off and I don't want to touch her because it stinks."
- "Her breath stinks too bad to kiss her. It's a turn off and it spoils the mood. I told her and she still ain't tryin' to do somethin' about it."

These are a few stories that couples share when they are bored and tired, and being real and want help. I have found that no one has a perfect spouse, perfect marriage, and every area of their marriage is blessed and most preciously holy than thou perfect and anointed without blemish. I do not believe this. Trust me, I don't believe you believe it either. From all of the stories and testimonies I have heard and more, there is always room for improvement, especially when we take the mask(s) off and be real. I encourage this for any couple. Keep it real. Keep it honest. Keep it open with one another about what hurts, what's troubling you, or what bothers you about them; whether in the bed or out of the bed. It is more harmful to hold things in, rather to get them out. If there is any flaw in the relationship, it will show up in the bed while making love. Actually, it will show up before the initial lovemaking, it will show up during foreplay.

Lovemaking should be a soul tied, covenant connection. This cannot happen when there is division. The Spiritual connected chain is broken and the seed is hindered. As a result, staying out all-night and leading on

Fruit & Toys Are Undefiled

to infidelity is the next step. To keep your marriage sparkling and both parties happy, take the time to find out what each other like rather than what they do not; without giving or sharing something that only you like without regards to the other. This is selfish and only leads to unfulfilled needs being met and to an unhappy marriage. Try new things. Open yourselves up to be as open as you can with your spouse, without making each other feel uncomfortable.

Fruit and toys are always fun and a way to be open, receive better orgasms and lasting turn on's. Hope this is not too loose for you. However, if we do not keep it real, more marriages will fail as a result of not being open and real about the unhappiness of the sex and relationship within the marriage. I have found that Christians have just as much, if not more of a divorce rate than the world do. This should not be so. Christian couples are supposed to set the example, the standard, and operate in a righteous, wholesome, covenant filled way that will lead sinners to want to change and turn towards the right way. Instead, Christian couples are too busy wearing the mask(s) and judging others who are kinky and spontaneous in their relationship. As a result, they go to worship at church or operate in ministry like nothing is wrong, and suddenly you see them vanish from the church setting. Soon after that, you find out that they got a divorce. This should not be so. I realize that marriage is a choice. Marriage is not for everybody. It is not mandatory for everyone to be marriage. In fact, Christ encourages us to remain single—married to Him. However, if you cannot abstain yourself, then marriage is the only option (1 Corinthians 7:7-8). This is not to cut down those who decide to marry, nor does it mean that it is wrong or I disapprove of it. I believe marriage is a beautiful thing. The only thing I will add is, if you are happier single, stay single. However, if marriage is happier for you, marry but make sure you are open, real, and giving it your all for life and not for pleasure and/or for a season. Too many are marrying only for pleasure, and for seasons, and are playing with lusty pleasure and not with real genuine God-felt love for the other spouse. Although looks (physical appearance) are a major plus, they eventually run out. Looks are to kill, but they are not everything. You must look deeper. You must search the Spirit within you both and see if there is a Spiritual connection within you two. The Word of God says, "try the spirits" to see if they are of God (1 John 4:1). There has to be a Spiritual covenant connection between the two, or this can be a number one hindrance.

For some that may still question using the toys and fruit after reading this chapter, in 1 Corinthians 7:4, it states that *"the wife has no power over her own body, but the husband: and likewise also the husband as no power over his own body, but the wife."* You both are under each other's rule and power. You two are <u>one</u> and as long as you two are in agreement, these additives are pure and can bring the power of intimate enjoyment in your marital spontaneity.

Scenario 1:

Jerry and Sue have been married for over 10 years and have been doing a lot of research on adding spontaneous things to their sex life. They are both Christian couples and want to make sure they keep it holy and acceptable to God on what they do to fulfill each other's sexual needs.

Jerry on the other hand is open to anything. He is tired of the same ol' things and the same ol' way, while Sue usually just wants to get it over with. Jerry and Sue have taken a whole new approach considering Jerry's attitude elsewhere—long hours of football nights, etc.

They both search the internet, magazines, tried talking to other couples, and last seeing a counselor with no help.

Just when they were about to give up, they were watching a movie, and in the movie, they were talking about adding fruit to their sex life. Jerry and Sue immediately tried it, and found it to be fun and very pleasing and helped to invite the mood and lead in to more pleasurable acts than when they both became very lazy and complacent. Jerry suggested trying different types of fruit they both like and Sue never disagreed. In fact, she was the first one to the door to go and buy the fruit.

The question is, how long do you think Jerry and Sue will last doing the fruit thing? Why did it take them so long to seek help for new pleasure to add to meeting each other's needs? Do you feel it was appropriate to use fruit in their intimate time? Was Sue really in agreement with Jerry at first on the idea? What else with the fruit could they have added to spruce up the fire in their relationship? Did they need to go and get help in this area, or should they two have come together and worked it out themselves? If you are married, will you try the fruit and toy idea? If you two have already tried it, how was it? How would you have handled the moment if this were you in this same position, either as Sue or Jerry, or as both? Why? And how? Write your answers below and if you are in a group, talk about it with them.

Fruit & Toys Are Undefiled

CHAPTER 14
We Are as One, Sex that Fulfills

As I have stated, the Bible clearly states that the bed is undefiled in previous chapters (Hebrews 13:4), sex is clean before God with your partner in marriage. In fact, God encourages sex between the married couple. God's desire was for them to be fruitful and to multiply (Genesis 1:27-28).

God created man and thought it was good that he have a helpmeet, a helpmate—A beautiful woman who would be by his side. As God brought them two together, His purpose was good; it was for them to satisfy one another totally and multiply. This means you two are as ONE. There is no control factor here. It is to please each other in such a way that you want and desire more.

As you two are one, there is no barriers between you two, and as you two join together in love making communion, you two become one in Spirit and in soul. You two are joined together with God's divine Will for the marriage.

This is not a strong experience; it should be very relaxing, passionate, and slow (taking your time). Not too strong with each other. And, as you two are passionately satisfying and fulfilling one another's needs and passionate desires, you are communicating, asking questions and making comments as your partner gives you confirmation. Like, "How you feel? How does this feel? Do you like that? Take it slow, don't rush. I want more. I like it that way." I encourage you to be determined to meet those questions and answers in every way possible. Take a look at the other chapters on this subject. They each give a more deeper and in depth study.

Because the bed is undefiled, meaning it is clean before God, you can be as spontaneous as you would like. There is no certain boundary as long as you two are in agreement, and it fulfills you two and makes your marriage stronger with one another, and in the Lord. Again, I give examples and further detail on this subject in the other chapters in the book. It should be one of your greatest desires to please your spouse and fulfill their every passionate needs. There are some Christian marriages that think that they should make love (have sex) with the Bible in their hands. Or, they feel that they should make love to the old musical classical or gospel hymns. There is no certain way you should fulfill each other, as long as you two are fulfilling, satisfying, and doing what keeps you two as one in the Lord. Nothing and no one else matters, nor are you two entitled to mimic the Jones's. Let the Jones's do it their way. I am not saying their way is wrong, however, it is about what works for their marriage and what makes them two happy. With this said, this is why it can become dangerous to ask other couples what they do in the bedroom to satisfy each other, because what they do and how they do it may not work for you and your spouse. It is best to pray about it, and if you choose to ask others, make sure what they tell you lines up with the Bible and what you and your partner want and needs. You can also listen to them but only use what works for you two, rather than try to do everything they do and mess up everything and be worse off than you two were before talking to them.

Scenario 1:

"I'm tired of not being fulfilled!" Peaches yells at George and slams the door. He has no strength to fight back. He's tired from her negative uncaring words, and from his condition. A year ago he found out that he was the problem of them not being able to have kids, and also he has a problem preforming and meeting Peaches sexual needs. Peaches is fed up and is coming close to leaving George.

She's told him over and over again that she is not being fulfilled, and could care less about his condition, and that she is real close to finding someone who can meet her needs.

The question is, why was Peaches so hard and had a lack of caring attitude? Why didn't she love and embrace her husband? Why didn't she seek help for his condition? Why didn't they both talk about maybe adopting a child? Why was George so passive about Peaches terrible attitude and yelling? Why didn't Peaches love George, embrace him, build him up, and be sensitive to his condition? Was Peaches patient to George's healing and possible change to getting help, or was she selfish, self-center, overbearing, and egotistical because she didn't have the condition he did? How would you have handled the moment if this were you in this same position, either as Peaches or George, or as both? Why? And how? Write your answers below and if you are in a group, talk about it with them.

We Are as One, Sex that Fulfills

15
CHAPTER
Opposites Attract

Have you ever heard that **opposites** attract? When you two are together there is a certain ray in which attracts you to that other person that you want, feel comfortable with, enjoy, and connect with. You want to spend all of your time with them. You two may not have much in common, but your like's work for the both of you. For example, take a football player who meets a woman who is an artist. The football player is really not into art, however, when he's around her, he enjoys her company so much that her personality makes him have an appreciation for the arts. Vice versa, the woman is not into football, however, when they two go to a football game, he makes her laugh and she has a good time cheering with him as everyone is cheering and agreeing on the same thing—winning the game. They are both attracted by each other's spirit as they both connect, regardless of being opposite. It is a give and take thing. Not all couples are willing to do this. It takes special people to do this. This is how opposites attract.

As you two are together and around other people, you may have heard, "man, those two are nothing alike. How did they meet?" Or, "how in the world do they get along, he's loud and she's quiet?" If they were to hang around you, you can clearly see that they two are special and that they are willing to do whatever it takes to please the other one. As they continuously do this, it builds their relationship and makes it stronger and stronger.

Often times, others may become jealous of your relationship because the connection between you and your spouse or soon to be spouse are so strong and connected. You have to be careful to guard your relationship and not allow others to dictate nor pass judgment, and continue to do what works for you both, although it may not please others or look right to them. It does not matter what they think. Only what you two think. Just do you and shut the door to nosey, jealous people.

Do not allow others to control you just because you two are different. For example, do not allow the football guys to tease you about going to an art exhibit and that it makes you look soft. Or, the other way around, do not allow other women who are super feminine to tease you about going to a rowdy football game and that you look and act like one of the guys. Absurd. Do what pleases you two and what you two like. There is nothing more beautiful when you two can compromise with joy and without any hidden agendas.

Scenario 1:

Jackie and Raymond hit it off from the first time they both laid eyes on each other although he is 5'5 and she is 5'10 and they have nothing in common. All of their friends stare, while some tease Raymond of being the short guy, making him the woman of the house and Jackie the man of the house in height.

They two hate their comments but do not care, they are madly in love with each other. She is a doctor and Raymond is a professional athletic trainer. This is another opposite area. They two work and agree on everything. In areas they two do not agree, they compromise as much as possible.

The question is, why is everybody hating on their relationship? Is it okay for a couple that is completely opposite and have nothing in common to make it? Is it anything wrong with a tall woman dating or marrying a short man? Will Jackie and Raymond make it and stay in agreement although they have nothing in common and are in two totally different career fields? After reading the scenario, do you feel they find something in common with the information provided? How would you have handled the moment if this were you in this same position, either as

Jackie or Raymond, or as both? Why? And how? Write your answers below and if you are in a group, talk about it with them.

CHAPTER 16
Financial Dysfunctionalism that Destroys the Vine

Almost all of the percentage of marital break ups are over financial dysfunctionalism. Dysfunctionalism in this arena defines as: not budgeting on one or both parts, she spends too much and on the wrong things, he spends too much and on the wrong things, did not consult with each other before spending money, lack of communication, non-caring behaviors, alcohol and substance abuse which caused an increase in debt, and immature decisions. These types of dysfunctionalisms are what destroy the Vine. They destroy the union and the bond between both married couples. They come to cancel communication, agreement, and financial stability within the marriage. Once this bond is destroyed, it is almost impossible to connect back together again, especially if the two do not come together and change them or do not seek help.

The "Vine" is the connection that only comes from God. The Vine is God (John 15:1-7, emphasis on verse 1, 4, and 5). He, the Vine, is the divine connection that guides the couple's relationship and helps them make the right financial decisions. Without the dependence on the Vine, the relationship perishes. As a result, emotional, verbal, and physical abuse, along with infidelity, ends up being the final result.

There has to be a line that every couple draws when it comes to finances. Working together is key to making this work. Winning together is another key to the couple making a committed decision to win together and keep out all of the negative setbacks and sidetracks that comes to destroy the relationship.

There should not be a control mechanism going on here. One person cannot control everything. There was a time when I was talking with some married couples and after our initial conversation, they departed but were still in the vicinity as we all were in a public gathering with several other people. As they were mingling, I heard God tell me the wife was controlling and that she wants to control everything. When one spouse wants to control everything and not allow their partner to have equal share, there is a problem and it is only a matter of time until the relationship will be tested with a lot of arguing, disagreement, confusion, and even separation to total break up. The only way it would remain is if the other spouse allows him or her to continue to control everything. This is why you may see a woman playing the man's role as a man plays the woman's role. For example, she is bossy and wants to cook only what she wants to eat every night, while never asking what the husband would like to eat. She wants everything cleaned just the way she wants it. She pays all of the bills in advanced when he feels that they could wait and pay them on time as other bills can be caught up first. He stays quiet and allows her to have her way on everything in order to keep peace and not get her upset. This is also the other way around with the man. This is dysfunctional. There is no way a person can last forever not saying anything and allowing the other spouse to control every single solitary thing. It is only a matter of time when he or she will explode and everything will come to the forefront.

You two must work together. You must come to an agreement on how to pay certain bills, what bills to pay and what bills to wait on; and compromise on what to cook each day. There is nothing wrong with asking your spouse what they would like to eat or have a taste for. This is an unselfish thing. You both are working together and helping one another. You may even cook one day or bring something home to eat. It is not always left up to one person to do everything. Eventually the guilty spouse will become burnt out and want to give up with false accusations that the innocent spouse doesn't do anything, when really it is the guilty spouse who is the controlling, dominating, and the guilty person who will not let them do anything. This is manipulation, domination, and control. These three words are not of God and come to curse the marriage with the result of a huge fight before break up. These same spirits also operate in other relationships, as it wants to control and dominate everyone and everything. Again, it is only a matter of time before disagreement or a great time bomb explodes. The only way it does not, is if everyone allows this person to control and have his or her way, which never lasts long.

There may be a time when you may lose your job and need to lean on your spouse's capital to make it through as you collect unemployment. This is not a time to ridicule or complain about why this or that is not done. You two should come together and talk about how you will adjust until things get back on the right track. This will eliminate the open door to constant fussing, separation, or even divorce.

When the Vine is broken, all contact, connection, and union is broken and has to quickly be united back together. It should be your goal to keep the Vine together and not allow piety things to break you two up.

"I am the true vine, and my Father is the husbandman."
John 15:1

"Abide in me, and I in you. As the branch cannot <u>bear fruit</u> of itself, except it abide in the vine; no more can ye, except ye abide in me."
John 15:4

"<u>I am the vine</u>, ye are the branches: He that abideth in me, and I in him, the same bringeth forth much fruit: for without me ye can do nothing."
John 15:5

Financial Dysfunctionalism that Destroys the Vine

Scenario 1:

Gary slams the bills down on the kitchen table while Tracie jumps as she prepares dinner in the kitchen. "I'm sick and tired of these bills that we cannot pay! Why didn't you tell me we are short this month?"

Tracie yells back, "I'm sick of you! I did tell you, you don't listen! Always yelling hot air and ain't gon' do nothin'!"

Tracie is sick of Gary's fighting every first of the month behind bills. Gary is sick of having to remember everything on his own, if not, nothing will get paid or done.

The both of them are in so much debt because Tracie will not listen and pay the bills on time, tell Gary that they do not have the money before they're due so that he can possibly seek other avenues, and she doesn't take being in the dark serious after their lights are cut off for non-payment.

They have to go to her parents, Gary's in-laws, which he is so embarrassed about and fed up. Her parents nag her about leaving Gary and blame everything on him secretly to Tracie. Their Spiritual connection is destroyed and the Vine is torn apart because of disconnection, lack of love, and negative and ineffective communication.

Tracie listens to her parents and soon divorces Gary without trying to work it out.

The question is, why didn't Gary stop yelling and talk calmly to Tracie, maybe she would have been able to receive him? Why didn't Tracie just listen to Gary considering she was the one who was wrong and had the problem? Why did she yell back when she was the one in the wrong? Why didn't they both come together and get a second job to help make ends meet? Why did Tracie allow her parents to control her and her marriage and talk her into divorcing her husband? Why did she listen to her parents and divorce her husband without trying to work it out? Do you consider Tracie to be controlling, dominating, and selfish? Was effective communication the key here? Was effective relationship building the key here? How would you have handled the moment if this were you in this same position, either as Tracie or Gary, or as both? Why? And how? Write your answers below and if you are in a group, talk about it with them.

Financial Dysfunctionalism that Destroys the Vine

CHAPTER 17
Relationships Matter

You should never go into a relationship having an attitude that nothing matters, or have a nonchalant, lackadaisical, and whatever attitude. Your relationship does matter. If it didn't, you would not have allowed yourself to get involved in one.

There are different types of relationships. One is marital, unmarried couple, friendship, sister to sister, brother to brother, niece and nephew, uncle and aunt, cousin and in-laws. I'm sure there are more, however, through the ones I have just mentioned, there is a bond in each of these within their own way. Each one should play a vital role in your life. It is one that you do not take lightly. You really care about them. You really cut for them. Therefore, the relationship you have with them matters.

There is not a no, it does not matter when you see them or if ever again. It should matter they should to.

Small things as well as big things matter. What is small to you, may not be small to him or her. Ask yourself, are you about small things or big things? Do they matter to you? You should never take it for granted that just because you want to keep the television on all night, every night, while you and your spouse is asleep, is no big deal, when it may be a big deal to your spouse because his or her sleep is distracted. This may seem petty to you, however, it is affecting your spouse's ability to wake up the next day, and them having to deal with your nonchalant control. You should take in consideration that it may not be him or her; it may be you not dealing with the habit and ability to compromise.

Another one is allowing your spouse to go out on a date with their ex quite frequently. You have this, it really doesn't matter attitude, and that he or she will be fine and that they're just friends. Again, it does matter. There should be a mutual respect, a place where you draw the line, and a great level of understanding so that the door does not open to negative things that can harm or divide your marriage and relationship.

Here is another example that is much different from what I have just talked about. There have been situations where I have seen the spouse feel as though his or her good is never good enough. You try so hard to please your spouse and never get a thank you or an appreciation. They always seem to forget your birthday and have to settle for a late one. They always seem to never agree to romance on a good day. They also act as if it does not matter on holidays that mean so much to you. They have this, it doesn't matter attitude in your relationship. This behavior will destroy the connection in the relationship. You have to understand that if it does not matter to you, nine times out of ten, it matters to your spouse. Do not take for granted that being late on his or her birthday is okay, especially when they always remember yours and are always on time. Do not take for granted that just because holidays do not mean much to you that it applies to everybody else, because it is a strong chance that they do not.

As you learn to appreciate your relationship more and more each day, the attitude of "my relationship doesn't matter" will change to "my relationship does matter". Let conviction be your change to appreciate your spouse and all he or she does with an attitude that he or she matters.

This not only applies to marriages, but also applies to all relationships (children, siblings, friendships, in-laws, family, etc.). It should mean something to you to think of your children, siblings, friendship, in-laws, cousin, etc. the way you would want them to love and think of you. You do not regard your spouse and forget about your children, siblings, friendship, in-laws, family, etc. They all should mean something to you as well.

Just because you are married does not mean you can disregard, neglect, or remove your family and friends. You are entitled to spend time with your family and friends as well as your husband. There should be a balance in your relationship while they all matter and they all have their equal share of pleasing.

Scenario 1:

It is Brenda's and Wayford's marriage anniversary and Brenda has gone all out in buying expensive gifts and a romantic dinner for two on a short one-day boat cruise. However, Wayford has this don't care attitude and feels that Brenda should know that he loves her and it does not take a bunch of gifts and a boat ride to prove it. Brenda on the other hand, thinks totally different. It matters to her. Not because she's a woman, but because she values her marriage and thanks God everyday for it and want to show her husband that it does matter, and how much he mean to her.

The night of the anniversary has arrived. Brenda and Wayford is out on the short boat cruise and Brenda has already given Wayford his gift while Wayford hands her nothing but says that he loves her and happy anniversary. Brenda is crushed and disappointed on the inside, but tries not to show it so that she wouldn't spoil the mood.

The question is, what happens next? Put your imagination to test. Why didn't it matter to Wayford? Why should remembering and appreciating Brenda and his marriage anniversary matter? Is it important to show it? Should Wayford have bought Brenda a gift and showed his appreciation?

Should Brenda had blown up and showed out on the boat? Should Brenda have given Wayford his gift considering he made no plans to give her one? Why is it important to show and know that things matter? Why is it important to show and know that your spouse matter? Why is it important to show and know that special people, your children, family, and friends matter? Was love an effective key here? Was appreciation an effective key here? How would you have handled the moment if this were you in this same position, either as Brenda or Wayford, or as both? Why? And how? Write your answers below and if you are in a group, talk about it with them.

Relationships Matter

18
CHAPTER
Fight to Make Up or Break Up?

Although there are fighting within relationships, the goal should not be to fight to make up or break up. This is very popular among couples who have no guidance and maturity. Most older and more seasoned couples are very settled and only want peace. However, there are situations where the seasoned couples are more set in their ways and willing to change, seems impossible. Moreover, after so many years of being together, the thought of breaking up is not an option. Unlike, most younger couples, they are more impatient and not willing to hang in there, so most of their fights are to break up rather than to make up.

No one wants to fight, but it does come and words are spoken that are detrimentally hurtful to both partners; and at times things fly across the room to show it. I have heard while counseling married couples that the best sex comes right after they fight. I often wondered how could that be true but as I thought about then, I can now say that that can be true. Most times after a fight, conviction sets in, and both or one of the couples begin to feel bad about what they said or did with the goal to make up is all that is on their mind. If you are a Christian and have a personal relationship with Christ, He will convict you when you say and do something wrong. I believe this is what brings couples back together. This also works for any couple, whether married or single.

God is not the author of confusion although confusion often comes and knocks at our doors, and attempts to use us to say and do devilish things that we should not say and do to one another (1 Corinthians 14:33). For example, there was a couple who had been married for quite some time. They had just went grocery shopping together and had gotten the groceries out of the car and were putting them away. The wife asked the husband what he wanted to eat and to set it aside so she could cook it. He set aside the pork chops and mentioned that he wanted them fried. She quickly makes a comment that she did not have a taste for fried pork chops. She had a taste for baked chicken because she was trying to get away from fried foods. The husband immediately blows up and says, "why did you ask me if you already made up in your mind what you were going to do in the first place?" She quickly and selfishly battled back with, "I hate I ever asked if I knew you were going to pitch a loud fit! You make me sick you fool!" Words became more intense, groceries flew in the air and up against the wall. He storms to the room threatening to leave. She encouraged him and dared him not to take a plate with him and hoped that he starves.

Three hours went by...
No food cooked. The entire house was quiet the entire time. During that time, conviction set in as they both are Christians and love the Lord dearly and want to please Him as well as each other so much. Their motives were so pure at first and never to hurt each other. However, as I said before, confusion will try to come and knock at the door and tear up every loving moment and environment it can. Because the devil loves confusion and fighting, he wants to tear up and separate a loving relationship.

He almost won until the Lord began to deal with them both and the husband went to her as she was sitting at the kitchen table still crying her eyes out. As he walked from around the corner and approached her, she immediately stood up and met his arms wrapping around her as she wrapped her arms around his. They both apologized for what was said and that it didn't matter what food was cooked, in fact, they even decided that going out to eat would be better.

They fought to make up rather than allow the devil to make them fight to end up in tragedy with a break up. This happens on a daily basis across America. It is important to have Jesus Christ within the relationship because when moments like this arise, it makes it easier for both partners to hear from the Holy Spirit, and allow Him to minister and to convict them to repentance.

In sharing time with your spouse, there are moments where you should compromise and be unselfish—pleasing the other rather than yourself. You please him, he will please you. You please her, she will please you. You two will be fulfilled.

There should be a give and take on both parts. Just as the wife asked the husband what he wanted to eat, that was a give and on his part was a take moment. However, she got careless and suddenly very selfish and turned her giving to taking only. She took back the blessing of giving and cursed it with taking to get what she wanted. He wanted fried pork chops after being asked, but she switched as if she never asked and wanted baked chicken because **SHE** was trying to get away from fried foods. It became a selfish moment for her because she asked him instead of just making dinner to fit them both. **SHE** turned it into her choice of dinner to fit her selfish desires only **AFTER SHE** asked him what he wanted to eat. That was very selfish on her part and opened the door of confusion to walk in and take root. It changed to entire atmosphere and attitudes. Words were said that should not have ever been said. Food went flying that should have been cooked and they both should have eaten alone at home and been happy. Hurt feelings and scars were manifested that should not have ever come. Remember you two are winning together, not winning alone.

This happens at every moment of your lives and at every minute of the day in your relationship. Trust me, these little foxes will destroy the Vine if they are not handled and stopped. What will happen is, the foxes will build up and build up and eat away at the relationship until they eventually grow and explode into something greater.

Married Christian couples are tied with secular married couples in divorces. This should not be so. Christian marriages should be setting the example for those of the world that do not desire to represent Christ within their marriage. However, this is not happening. Some Christian marriages act more worldly than secular (worldly) marriages. Christians have to turn this around and allow Christ to **be the center** of their relationship and **not the outsider**. Christ wants to come in and dwell within the Christian marriage. He wants to be the center of the relationship. He wants to make all of the decisions and set the pace for the marriage and family (if any). Christian couples must set the example of how a Godly marriage should operate on a daily basis.

There was another couple who fought all the time. In fact, more than they got along. They actually fought before they got married. But was so in love, that they decided that marriage was the best choice. Well, it wasn't a good idea. They fought so much that they could and would not agree on anything the other one said or did. If she said the sky is blue, he disagreed and said it's green. If he said he wanted to ride a horse, she would say riding a pony is better. Just very negative and no change for unity and love to shower them. Affection was hardly ever there for them both. It would seem that they would be satisfied with that but they were not. They wanted to be loved and satisfied but did not find it fulfilling. Within every relationship, we all know that affection is very important and should not be treated selfishly. We all want to be loved and touched at times. Without love and affection, emotional separation, depression, anger, agitation, and impatience will set in. If this fits your relationship, you should come together and decide whether being together is feasible. And, if you two make the choice to be together, counseling must be a choice for the both of you. If you choose not to get counseling, much prayer and fasting has to be the highlight of the relationship until things, feelings, emotions, attitudes, clashing personalities, negative comments, inner hatred comes out and is no longer a part of your lives.

Most times, I have found that couples like this really have nothing to do with the negative ways and feelings they have with each other. It has to do with what is going on within their own individual hearts, minds, and spirits. They have not forgiven, or something has happened to them in their past or as a child (molested, raped, or abused) that does not have anything to do with their spouse. The spouse happens to be the victim because the one who is hurt has not let the past go and have not released the hurt. As a result, the root is not that they cannot get along, the root is the fact that they need to be healed from their own individual past, hidden hurts and iniquities.

You may ask, "how do I release the root?" I will answer:

1. **Admit.** First admit to yourself, your spouse, and to God that you have a problem and need to be healed.
2. **Repent.** You should then repent for hurting your spouse and others who have been affected by your negative, selfish actions and attitude (Acts 3:19).

3. **Release.** You must release the hurt, the pain, depression, oppression, suicidal thoughts, unforgiveness, areas where you are not satisfied within yourself and your marriage, and areas where you do not like yourself and make it your point to make your spouse and others unhappy (Isaiah 53:5).
4. **Wait.** You should then wait for God to heal and uproot those areas that need to come out (Isaiah 40:31).
5. **Make it a point.** Now that you are free by the Holy Spirit and by the renewing of your mind, you should make it a point to make your spouse and others happy every chance you get. Remember always to walk in love and to appreciate your relationship(s) and show your spouse the new positive, free you on a daily basis (John 8:36).

Forgive to be Forgiven, Forgiven to Forgive

There is a constant fight across the globe and in every relationship to forgive someone who has hurt you, whether one second of hurt or fifty years of hurt. Forgiveness works all the same, even for those who hurt you and you don't even know them. I have found that it is worse in relationships. The closer they are to you, to greater the hurt. In this case, guarding your mouth and watching what you say and do is very important. You do not want to be considered the victor, versus the victim. It is easy to say, "someone hurt me" rather than to say, "I hate I hurt him or her". No one wants to give an account for their actions but is quick to slain and slaughter others, either by mouth or by actions. We must recognize as Christian Believers when we are in error (2 Peter 3:17). And, if we make a mistake, we should run to that person to get it right by asking for forgiveness. You must forgive to be forgiven. And you must understand that Jesus Christ forgave you of your sins, so that is all the more reason why you need to forgive—forgiven to forgive (Colossians 1:14).

I realize this is a touchy subject when it comes to you having to forgive those who have hurt you, rather its one minute of hurt or fifty years of hurt. Your spouse is no different than those who hurt you in other relationships or with those who you are not close to. It seems to hurt worse when your spouse hurts you or when your child or children hurt you if you have any. You want to leave them alone right away and in some cases you never want to see them again until you sober up and realize that the fight wasn't really even that big of a deal. However, there are some cases when the fight really is big and getting over it seems impossible. This is when you have to remember that you must forgive. I'm sure the thought(s) will always be there, but as time goes on and as you release the hurt, the thought(s) will leave to. I am reminded of Peter, one of the disciples in the Bible who asked Jesus how many times should we (Christians) forgive, and Jesus answered him by saying, seventy times seven times a day. That is a lot when you think about it. However, just as you have to forgive him or her, they have to forgive you that many times as well. It works both ways. And, here is another dagger, it does not matter how great of the hurt they did to you, and the small hurt you did to them, or vice versa, it is all still the same to God. You still forgive.

Fight to Make Up or Break Up?

Sorry, but this is true. I'm sensitive to those who have been hurt whether on a small or greater degree. And, I know how it is being in a relationship where they hurt you and felt as if they did not do anything wrong. Hurt is hurt, and hurting someone is hurting someone. However, what helped me to realize on the other end is that I must forgive them because I two have made mistakes against people and wanted so badly for them to forgive me. Jesus helped me to realize that it all works the same. You have to forgive in order that someone else will forgive you when you make mistakes against them (Matthew 18:21-22).

Relationships break up so quick when it comes to hurt. The relationship is torn apart, while either leaving them both in the same house acting as if they do not even know each other, or leaving them two in constant heated battles of, "when you hurt me, and this and that and that and this." "I won't forget what you did to me" "I can't forgive you," "I don't want to see you again and soon I'm leaving." And, the list goes on and on. Your goal should be to win in every area of your marriage and relationship(s). You do not look to fight just to make up. You should always look to love and to please, this will delete all the drama you will have to go through if you do not.

Scenario 1:

Tommy has worked at a strip club as a bartender for over six years. The environment was the norm for him and he desired no woman other than his beautiful wife Sheila he had waiting on him at home every night. He was tested on a nightly basis, but never gave in because he loved Sheila so much.

Although his faithfulness was true by his word, Sheila was still hesitant to believe. A strip club? Full of naked women? Provocative dancing and coming up to you with evil lust? Yea' right. What Sheila failed to realize is that she met him after he became a bartender in the strip club so she already knew his profession.

She couldn't wait to fuss and fight about other women, especially when she smelled what smelled like perfume on his clothes after he arrived home every night from work.

The question is, why did Sheila choose to marry Tommy after knowing his profession as a bartender at a strip club? Why was she still insecure when he explained to her that she was the only one he loved? Was Sheila wrong for being a little leery? Was Sheila wrong for fussing and fighting with Tommy considering he told her the truth? Should Tommy had left Sheila alone? Should Tommy had left Sheila considering he told her the truth and she still acted insecure and did not trust him? Should Tommy have looked for a new job to please the fact that Sheila was uncomfortable with his profession, for the sake of his marriage? Do you believe they should be together? What do you think happens next? Put your imagination to test. Was trust the effective key here? How would you have handled the moment if this were you in this same position, either as Sheila or Tommy, or as both? Why? And how? Write your answers below and if you are in a group, talk about it with them.

Fight to Make Up or Break Up?

CHAPTER 19
The Popularity of Divorce:
Break the Repeating Curse

> **Control:** *To exercise authoritative or dominating influence over; direct. Having a need to control other people's behavior.*
> **Submission:** *accept or yield to a superior force or to the authority or will of another person. To subject to some kind of treatment or influence.*

The Popularity of Divorce have become like eating a box of your favorite chocolates and can't stop. It has even become like watching the latest Springer Show and all the drama it entails with married couples yelling, shouting, fighting and scratching each other's eyes out after hearing the blatant naked truth of infidelity or even worse. The cycle must stop.

Breaking the Repeating Curse

You must break the repeating curse. If divorce runs in your family, you must be determined to break the curse. If infidelity runs in your family, you must be determined to break the repeating curse. Breaking the repeating curse is done best through communication, dedication, and prayer. It is done by working together and making a commitment to be honest and true to each other and refuse to follow in your mother's, father's, or grandparent's footsteps of this painful generational curse.

Communication works alongside working together with not just one person in the relationship controlling everything. It takes communication to make the marriage work. Although it is true that the man is the head of the household according the Bible, he and the wife has to work together in order to make the marriage work successfully and effectively (Ephesians 5:23). The man in the marriage may not feel as if he has to tell his wife everywhere he goes, and the wife feels the same. As I have counseled marriages, this has been a pet peeve in the marriage. The spouse feels that the other spouse is over possessive and overbearing when they have to tell them where they are going all the time. I say, if there is no communication, there is no relationship. If there is no relationship, there is potential to open the door to other people to intervene in the relationship the wrong way. Communication works best when it is handled with the right attitude and Spirit. It should be given in regards to accountability with a positive Godly attitude, rather than negative control to keep the other spouse in check (Philemon 1:6). It is not a game. Marriage is work, but it is rewarding when there is understanding, respect, and communication upfront and remains that way throughout the marriage. The generational curse will be broken.

Dedication is also a main factor in the marriage and relationship. The question to ask yourself is, "Am I dedicated?" "What am I dedicated too?" "Do I really love my spouse enough to be dedicated in every area of our marriage and relationship?" If you can answer each of these questions effectively, you are well on your way. You will be considered a dedicated spouse. If you are dating and contemplating marriage, dedication will get you there. It is the number one key to a successful relationship and will not work any other way. When you are dedicated to your spouse, you are showing a positive, life lasting example to your spouse, child or children (if any), and even to other marriages that are watching you as an example.

Prayer will bring a marriage together and will keep it together (Colossians 4:2). Most Christian Marriages fail across the world because there is no prayer going forth in the relationship. Some marriages do not care to pray because everything seems to be going their way. To make a relationship last by only the human physical strength of the two spouses will run out, especially when test and trials come up against the marriage; and against them individually. You will need the strength of the Strong Tower, which is Jesus Christ Himself to help you when those trying times arise (Proverbs 18:10). Neither one of us can ever make it alone without God. He should be the center of the marriage and the relationship.

Un-Satisfaction Will Tear a Marriage Union to Pieces

There are millions of unhappy, unsatisfied marriages all across the globe. Most hate they ever got married. They looked for love in all the wrong places. The lust of their eyes made the decision to marry. She looked good and had all the curves in all the right places. He was fine and his body was one that you did not want anybody else to have. His or her conversation was one you couldn't get away from. You two were caught up in, "I gotta' have em' before somebody else take em'." But now, you're hoping someone else come and take em'.

Now you two have been married for ex amount of years and it seems as if you're trapped in a dark closet with no way out. You can't take a step for her watching your every move. She can't go to the store to buy groceries for you secretly following her. Un-satisfied with your marriage will make you do possessed, obsessive, obscene things such as this. Marriage is not supposed to be set-up as this. There should not be any kind of checking up on him 24-7, nor should there be any following her everywhere she goes. Marriage is honorable and full of respect and trust. These types of examples I just shared are not trust nor are they exemplifying respect.

It does not always have to be big things that will tear a marriage apart. Small things can also, such as:

1. Constantly keeping a dirty bathroom and bedroom (dirty sheets and underclothes and clothes everywhere).
2. Allowing the dog or cat to urinate and poop all over the house or apartment and never cleaning it.

3. Not bathing regularly. It is hard to be romantic with a dirty and stinky spouse.
4. Stinky breath.
5. Not cooking regularly—never buying any groceries to cook and not cooking at all.
6. Out partying all night and all through the week.
7. Spending time with friends and never any time with your spouse.

There are many more, but too many to add in this book. These seem to be small things, but they are huge when repeated over and over and over again. They become so overwhelming that huge fights have blown up and have escalated to more dangerous situations. This type of constant behavior causes separation and even divorce. You should work hard every day to satisfy your spouse as much as you can. This will bring a fruitful relationship and one that is ever lasting.

Control -vs- Submissiveness

There is a tug a WAR going on between the spirit of control and a submissive spirit. They two want to be in control (Galatians 5:17). One wants to have complete ownership over the other. The spirit of control seeks to devour anybody who does not give it its way, stands up against it, or even the other way around—too nice and says yes to everything. A person who operates in a spirit of control watches and studies those who are weak, too nice, or can see an immediate open door to control him or her. When they cannot get their way, they will disrupt and will attack those where they are weak in order to gain control. The guilty person operating in this spirit will control the spouse to get their way all the time and make them do everything. When the innocent spouse becomes tired, worn out, and angry, the guilty spouse who is operating in this spirit will cry and make the innocent spouse feel guilty; when he or she is really innocent and turns and gives them their way anyway.

A submissive spirit is just the opposite. It seeks to do right and keep peace in every situation and within the relationship. It seeks to do the Will of God and always strive to make things better, peaceful, and right. There is never an end to this vicious cycle until the guilty party makes up in his or her mind that they will no longer allow this spirit to control them and make them treat others in such a negative and hateful way.

There are times when operating in the spirit of control in any relationship, him or her manipulates and intimidates the spouse and makes them afraid and tries to weaken them with the force of their words and actions. You may be one who is guilty of this, and feel that you are not wrong and do not realize that you are operating in this way. Or you may feel that it is normal and the power that you have over everybody feels right and that it's okay. For example, you and your spouse and children (if any) are currently moving into your new home and YOU forcefully say exactly where YOU want the furniture to go, not having any regards to anyone's opinion. Your spouse is now making dinner; he or she has baked chicken instead of frying it. You disagree and demand that he or she fry the chicken. The sheets on the bed are a neutral color for the both of you but you do not like the color so you demand that he or she change it to all black. Everything must be your way or it will not work and you will make everybody unhappy. Your spouse is very unhappy, the kids are very unhappy because of the fighting, disagreement, cursing, and yelling all over the house. These examples are given to help you realize and identify that there is a problem and if you are operating in those areas I have just provided, you are in error and should seek immediate change. Satan has blinded your eyes to think that you are right when in fact you are wrong. Control is a very strong spirit and is not an easy thing to break, especially when you have had it all of your life. It can be very abusive; which in most cases throughout the world is how and why murder, restraining orders, or even long years in prison have come about. The only way this spirit can be broken in your life is by much prayer, fasting, confessing that you have a problem, repenting to God and to others you've hurt, confessing that you are healed, and by constant counseling until it is completely broken. It is in your faith the amount of time it will take you to be healed. It can be done quickly, or it can take a very long time.

The spirit of control is the devil's way of keeping you blind and bound in order to keep you away from a beautiful happy life and relationship. Make a decision today to admit that you need help and that this is a problem in your life and relationship, and allow God to help you. You are well on your way to a happy life you always wanted. Your spouse will be happy and your children, if any, will be also.

What a Spirit of Control Carries:	
• Jealousy	• Cheating
• Hatred	• Physical Abuse
• Dishonesty *(lies)*	• Mental Abuse
• Infidelity	• Emotional Abuse
• *Disobedience*	• Verbal Abuse
• Do not want to see anyone happy but yourself	• Pride
	• Selfishness
• Constant drama and pain	• Mental Disorder
• Seeks to be in control over every situation and person	• Manipulation
	• Domination
• Do not want to see others shine, even those who have helped and loved you	

As I have stated before, a submissive spirit is just the opposite of the spirit of control. Submissiveness seeks to be a peacemaker. It seeks to please at all times. This is how God seeks to do in our lives and in every relationship. It does not take pleasure in confusion and abuse. In fact, it is recommended through the Word of God that every relationship operate in this way. Both parties must have a humble and contrite spirit (Proverbs 16:19, 29:23). You two must have submissiveness operating at all times, and not just demanding or expecting one to up hold this by themselves. This is not fair. Both of you are responsible. Not just one. You both are ONE and have to operate as ONE. Work together and not apart and divided. A house that is divided will fall (Matthew 12:25). It cannot stand. And divorce is the next option along with abuse.

What a Submissive Spirit Carries:

- Love
- Humbleness
- Giving
- Peace
- Joy
- Unselfishness
- Truth
- Unity
- Constant pleasing
- Kindness
- Helps
- Order *(knowing your place)*
- Submit
- Willingness
- Compassion

You should strive to carry these things listed on the chart above in your relationship on a daily basis. This will keep out the hateful demon of control that do not want to see you, your spouse, your marriage, your family, your kids (if any), or your friends happy in every way.

Scenario 1:

Jared and Jackie just arrived at a restaurant he always choose when he and Jackie go out to eat for dinner. Jackie never chooses the restaurant, for that matter, she never even chooses what she wants to eat. Jared always makes all of the decisions for her. They have been married for two years.

The fact that she was raised up in a God-fearing family where she is a PK kid—meaning she is the child of her parents who are pastors and co-pastors of a local church, she was always taught to submit to her husband and that he is always in control and is always right.

Jared has taken complete control and advantage of this submission. Jackie cooks, fixes his plate, and most times seconds. She always cooks his favorite meals, in which is almost never what she wants. She makes his lunch for work. She runs his bath water just the way he wants it. She is the one who does the most pleasing as she and him make love, he does not make it a priority to please her. And, whenever he does just a little bit, he is way too rough. She never talks over him, always quiet and waits for her time to speak, if at all.

Out of all this, Jared is not satisfied and is negative about everything Jackie does. He yells for nothing, especially if there is anything that looks out of place. He curses her out. He talks down to her—"you're ugly and fat! That's why don't nobody want you!" "You're a sorry excuse for a wife and I shouldn't have married you!"

One day, Jared couldn't wait to get fired up about the fact that Jackie made his bath water way too hot. He kicks her out and sends her to her parent's house.

As Jackie arrives at her parent's house with all of her things, she walks in to her father doing the same thing to *her mother. Although her father is the pastor of the church, his control is hidden behind the walls of their house.*

Jackie's mother runs to her for aide as her father follows and yells, "you can leave right back out the door with yo' sorry daughter! I can't count on you to make a bed up, fix my dinner the way I want it, wash my car clean, I can't count on you to do nothin'! I'm better off finding me a woman who I know can take care of my needs!"

Jackie's mother cries hysterically in her arms as Jackie's father grabs her clothes, throws them out on the porch, and demands that she leaves with Jackie.

He has made plans to file for divorce.

The question is, is Jared out of line for choosing the restaurant and making all of the decisions without Jackie having a say so? Was Jared wrong for choosing Jackie's meals every time they went out for dinner? Was Jared right for getting mad at everything Jackie does? Have Jared taken advantage of the way a husband and a wife should biblically operate in marriage? Was Jackie's dad out of line for getting mad and treating Jackie's mother as Jared treats Jackie? Is her dad a hypocrite for telling the church how they should act but secretly does the opposite (controlling and abusive) to his wife? Does Jackie's dad have an abusive controlling problem? Should Jackie's dad divorce his wife or should the wife divorce the dad, or should they both seek counseling? Is the dad's reason legitimate? Do you think Jared and Jackie's dad is operating under a generational curse that has been handed down to them by their fathers or grandfathers? Is Jackie and her mother considered weak for their submission to their husbands? Does Jackie and her mother have the right submission that is stated in the Bible, or are they two over board? Is fear a factor here? Why didn't Jackie and her mother stand up to their husband's? Do you think they should have? Do you believe they all should be together? What do you think happens next? Put your imagination to test. How would you have handled the moment if this were you in this same position, either as Jared, Jackie, Jackie's father or mother, or as all of them? Why? And how? Write your answers below and if you are in a group, talk about it with them.

_____

_____

_____

_____

_____

_____

_____

_____

_____

_____

_____

_____

The Popularity of Divorce

Scenario 2:

Patricia is the supervisor at a Chemical Plant in the city. Her high position keeps her coming home late even though she and her husband Kevin have a child that needs special attention. Patricia feels that it is not her duty to tend to their special needs child considering he is a boy and fathers should see after boys. She also believes that his duties are not much and can be handled when she gets home late from work.

Kevin is totally committed although he has a nine to five job himself and has to race to daycare after work, pick up their special needs child, and race home to prepare the house for the night for his child; and hopefully for Patricia that comes in late after work.

Patricia's boss over her has just offered her a better position in the company with more money and less hours. She'll be able to come home early in the afternoon and have time for her son and take care of Kevin. She is undecided.

The question is, is Kevin's needs being met? Why does Patricia feel that she does not have to do anything to help Kevin at home and with their special needs child? Is she making the right decision? Is Patricia and Kevin really in love? Are they really committed to each other and their marriage? Is it Kevin's duty to be the only one seeing after their special needs son? Why is Patricia so lazy and want things her way? Do you consider her controlling? Do you consider Kevin controlling? Do you consider Kevin a good dad? Should Kevin put his foot down and tell Patricia the truth about her controlling ways? Should and will Patricia take the higher position offered to her? What do you think happens next? Put your imagination to test. How would you have handled the moment if this were you in this same position, either as Kevin or Patricia, or as them both? Why? And how? Write your answers below and if you are in a group, talk about it with them.

_____

_____

_____

_____

_____

_____

_____

_____

_____

_____

The Popularity of Divorce

Scenario 3:

Marie and Joe have a nineteen year old son, Joe Jr. who stays out way past his curfew. He has no job and does not want to do anything with his life. His room is always filthy with dirty clothes laying everywhere, dirty dishes he's brought and left in his room for weeks, and has naked photos of swim suit and porn models pinned up on the walls that he has been told numerous of times to take down. Joe Jr. has no regards to listening and respecting Joe's and Marie's authority. Joe is constantly in a verbal fight with him and each time he threatens to kick him out, Marie begs Joe not to.

Later, Joe tells Marie in their room that Joe Jr. is controlling her and that he just wants his way and wants to run her and their household. Marie denies it and almost blames Joe for Joe Jr's. actions, and that he has no right to falsely accuse Joe Jr. If he would be a better father, Joe Jr. would do better.

When Joe is not home, Marie goes to the mall and shops with Joe Jr. treating him like he is her husband, and buying nothing for Joe. Marie secretly gives Joe Jr. money and cleans up his room, and later tells Joe that Joe Jr. cleaned his room up himself. Joe later finds out that Joe Jr. did not clean his room up and is fed up with Marie babying Joe Jr.

This has been going on throughout their marriage and Joe cannot take it anymore.

Joe is furious and demands that Marie and Joe Jr. change or he's filing for divorce.

The question is, is Marie out of line for siding with Joe Jr.? Should Joe Jr. be out on his own at nineteen? Should Joe Jr. have a job or be in school? Why did Joe have to tell Marie that Joe Jr. was controlling her and their household, should she have seen that herself? Is she in denial? Why did Marie side with Joe Jr.? Shouldn't she have sided with her husband? Is Marie submitted to her husband or is she submitted to her son Joe Jr.? Do Marie have her priorities mixed up with treating her son like her husband by shopping for him instead of shopping for her husband Joe? Do you think Joe Jr. is babied and Marie baby's him? Do you consider Joe Jr. controlling or do you consider Joe controlling? Should Joe file for a divorce or should they all seek counseling to work their situation out? What do you think happens next? Put your imagination to test. How would you have handled the moment if this were you in this same position, either as Joe, Marie, or Joe Jr., or as them all? Why? And how? Write your answers below and if you are in a group, talk about it with them.

_____

_____

_____

The Popularity of Divorce

The Popularity of Divorce

CHAPTER 20
Present But not Connected

This chapter brings such a profound role on a relationship that is not where it should be. A marriage is supposed to be a unified bone to bone, flesh to flesh connection (Genesis 2:23). You should be able to look at your spouse and love being around them. You should be able to look at your spouse and appreciate who they are. Have you ever felt alone while around your spouse?

To be present with someone, but not connected is the most horrible feeling one can ever encounter. God would never place you with someone you are not connected and compatible with, unless you were not specific when you made your request. It is important to be specific while praying for what type of mate you want. If you are feeling some disconnected types of feelings and are operating in some type of withdrawn way within your marriage, you should reevaluate why you got married in the first place. Immediate prayer is a must as you seek God for direction on why you feel the way you do, open up and talk and be honest with your spouse. You two should come together and ask each other why you two are having those types of feelings and disconnection. God is faithful. And He is faithful with His promises for the marriage. If you two desire to be together, God will make every way possible for you two to identify what the problem is, give direction on how to solve it, and the patience, faith, and wisdom on how to change and work on them. Once these areas are practiced, your disconnection should leave and your connection should begin connecting together.

If there are unethical feelings within your relationship after God brought it together, you can guarantee that the devil (satan) has a hand in it. The devil will always try to destroy or bring confusion where there is connection. He does not want you two connected because then you two will have too much power and he will be destroyed.

Many times couples only look at the fleshy (outer appearance) of what is going on, rather than what is happening on the inside (in the spiritual realm). There is a constant fight in the spiritual realm (within). The Word of God says that the flesh wars against the Spirit and the Spirit wars against the flesh (Galatians 5:17). The devil is warring against everything that the Lord has promised you and your husband or wife. If you two are destined to do a great and mighty work here on the earth, he is against it. If you two are purposed to work in ministry together, the devil is against it. If you two are purposed to travel the world and speak to the hearts of many, the devil is against it. If you two are good at making a difference in the lives of other relationships and individuals, the devil is against it. And because of this, in areas where you were once happy with your spouse when you two first got married or dated before you got married, and now when you look at him or her, you cringe on the inside because you are now unhappy. Please know who is responsible for this. It is the devil. Before making the fleshy assumption that it is your spouse, look at who is really trying to destroy the covenant and the purpose you two have.

This is also for a friendship and family relationship. God does not make mistakes, we may make mistakes, but God will never make a mistake nor will He ever change His promise, covenant, and plan. And, God will never start something that He cannot finish (Philippians 1:6). God would never call you with someone who you are not compatible with, nor will He ever team you up with someone who cannot help you fulfill your God given assignment. Most times, the assignment is Spiritual and the mission that God has given you two to complete is not in how cute you two look together. So please go back to God through prayer and check and see if you two are divinely purposed to be married or together. Many times, we get in a hurry and miss God and yet think that because everything is going good at first, it had to be God who connected you two together. However, when all hell breaks loose, you question and begin to see that it was never God who placed you two together, it was emotions and the struggle of outer attraction that brought you two together. Remember, trials will come within your relationship and covenant partnership. And yes, God may be the One Who placed you two together, but when it is truly Him, He will always give you two the grace, knowledge, endurance, love, passion, forgiveness, long suffering, and peacemaking to endure with that person or spouse. The outcome will always be victorious.

Most times, you should not look at them, but look at yourself. I was counseling a family who had a troubled teen and I asked the question, "what are you two having trouble with?" The first answer that was given was regarded towards the other one rather than towards themselves. No one wants to take responsibility for his or her own actions. No one wants to mount up to when they are wrong. And, no one wants to apologize for their wrong. There is no way that marriage will last long. It is only a matter of time when that relationship will deteriorate. It often saddens me when I see married couples who are supposed to be together can't get along or get a divorce. This happened as a result of them not being strong enough to see that the devil was on their trail, and sent demonic darts against them because he knew they were not praying nor praying for one another. A relationship that does not pray together and for each other, will open the door for the devil to attack their relationship and work against every area they are weak in. Once he is done within these areas, the relationship is left naked, exposed to demonic attacks and let downs. If you choose to be married, you must fight for your relationship.

Do not get involved in something that God has not called; it will be hell for you to keep. However, when you wait on the Lord, He will give you everything you need to defeat the devil, and give you and your spouse the victory in every area the devil will try to destroy. God will win the battles the devil sends against your relationship. The Bible speaks, *"Whom the Lord has put together, let no man put asunder"* (Matthew 19:6). What this means is, who God has put together, let no man tear them a part.

Here With me, But Your Mind is in Another Place

Have you ever met a person whose physical appearance seems to be shunned away from having any interest in you and communication seems totally disoriented? That person is physically present with you, but their heart, mind, spirit, and attitude is many miles away from you? This is what I am speaking of when I make this statement and the highlight of this chapter.

Both partners are presently spending time together but there is no connection among them. There must be a physical, mental, emotional, and spiritual connection between the two for it to work. If not, you two must have a talk as to why there is a disconnection and make final decisions on either an outlet, or how to come up with an agreement to connect or reconnect. Most times prayer and counseling is appropriate if an agreement cannot be made among the two.

Scenario 1:

Ray and Doris have been married for five years and are at the local beach in their city gazing into each other's eyes. It appears that they two are in love and nothing and no one can keep them apart. Their marriage seems connected and inseparable.

Doris's heart, mind, attitude, and thoughts are many miles away as she can't stop thinking about a nice guy she met on her job as they travel weekly to another city on a job assignment. Ray holds Doris in his arms and attempts to kiss her but notices that she is a little skeptical but tries to hide it. He asks, "what's wrong?" she quickly comes back with, "I'm tired from work."

They decide to travel back home and turn in so she can get some rest.

The question is, is Ray and Doris truly connected? Is Doris truly in love with Ray or is she in love with someone else—the guy on her job? Although Ray and Doris is physically together, is there sweet connection happening there at the beach? Is the devil on his evil assignment to destroy their marriage? Is Doris really tired from work or is it an excuse to ruin the mood? What do you think happens next? Put your imagination to test. How would you have handled the moment if this were you in this same position, either as Ray or Doris, or as them both? Why? And how? Write your answers below and if you are in a group, talk about it with them.

_____

_____

_____

CHAPTER 21
The Pain of Infidelity:
The Healing Process

The pain of infidelity is always a sensitive subject to speak about. In fact, it is a dagger in one's heart. If you are a victim, it can break you down in so that you don't want to live. There have been cases where the marriage has never been restored. It is a matter of choice to continue on with the guilty one staring you in the face. There are many remedies and opinions on how to handle this, but I can say that it is different with each person and each relationship and with each situation.

There are cases where the couple dealing with this have filled the atmosphere with anger, hatred, unforgiveness, resentment, and fear. It was worse as children were involved. One may ask how in the world can a marriage be saved from the pain of infidelity? The only answer that can be given would be for both partners to make a decision on whether or not they are going to try to make it work, or let it go. It is a conscious and committed decision on both sides. Again, there may be many remedies, opinions, marital books, or counseling sessions on the matter, however, it all boils down to the actual two who are in that situation and what they two agree to do. The Word of God states that the person who commits adultery frees the other to leave and to divorce (Matthew 19:9).

It is important to strive to have a strong passion-filled relationship with one another in order to rebuild a marriage that has been left in ruins of infidelity. If this is not the case with the two of them, it will not last. They will both part and go their separate ways. There has to be a willingness to forgive completely (remembering the past no more), to rebuild, and to stick it out until the marriage is back complete and fulfilled.

The Healing Process

Healing is available for many different reasons. Healing is the process of making healthy again. In this case, I am speaking of making spiritually whole again. When infidelity is fresh, most women and men do not want to talk or see the guilty spouse, do not want to talk to anyone, do not want phone calls, do not want any advice, do not want to be hugged, do not want to forgive, and do not want to be healed from the pain of the situation. They suffer from rejection, resentment, and the torment of fear.

In this painful time, there is still healing for you. Make your healing for yourself. If you think about doing it for the other party, chances are it will not get done, at least no time soon. When we are not able to heal ourselves, God is waiting to do all of the work. He knows what you are going through and He is the only One who can heal deep within to a point where you will feel a deep, mighty release from within. I encourage you to go deep and allow God to pull up the hurt so that you can get **YOU** back and be free to go on.

The scripture, James 5:16 states *"to confess your faults one to another, pray for another, that you may be healed. The effectual fervent prayer of a righteous man availeth much."* At times when we are hurt, we try to handle it alone with no help. However, I have learned that some hurts are much too strong and much too great for us to handle alone. We need someone else or others to talk to. We need them to help us to vent and to release it. I realize the trust factor plays a big part in releasing to others. However, in this case when the pain is much too great for you to handle, it is imperative to get additional help. Once you find that someone who you can vent and talk too, pray with, and totally let go, you will be glad that you did. There is nothing like being totally free from being bound from the pain caused by another person. There are many other sources that can help toward your healing, but the ultimate help and Healer is the Almighty God Himself. This is what He specializes in. He will direct you through His Holy Spirit on who you can talk to and who you can release to.

As you release your hurt, pain, and anger to God, it gets better in time. It is most times a process. As time goes on, your love will be restored and you can then move on with your life. You can also forgive him or her for what they have done and move on within yourself.

What are your thoughts on this?

_____
_____
_____
_____
_____
_____
_____

You Must Choose to Forgive

There is not an option to forgive, but there is an option as to whether or not to stay in that relationship (Matthew 18:21-22).

We all have done things that we are not proud of. It works the same in any relationship we may encounter. In this case, it works the same in a marriage who has or is suffering from infidelity. When you choose to forgive, you must completely let it go. Often times the spouse who is innocent tries to let the pain of the incident go without totally forgiving and releasing that person from their past actions. The innocent one brings up every single thing they did wrong to them and constantly reminds them of the pain and the hurt they took them through. The guilty one is caught with so much guilt and conviction to a point where it is unbearable for them to remain and call it quits.

When you make up in your mind that you are no longer going to carry him or her and what they did, you can be free to love them and get back the wholesome, loving, passion-filled marriage you have ever had. It will be better than it has ever been.

Choose to Stay or Choose to Leave
As I have stated above, you have a choice to stay and a choice to leave. If you do not completely let go of the past and the pain of their infidelity, you are cheating yourself and them and the purpose to stay is a waste of time. I say this because you will always make him or her remember what they did, constantly remind them how you cannot completely forgive them, looking at him or her is unbearable, and constantly asking them why did they do what they did. Years have gone by and the same conversation and questions are being asked. Constantly watching them and accusing them of cheating when they are not. The purpose and plan to let the past go and begin to rebuild your marriage will not be a success due to these examples. Choose to stay or choose to leave.

Unfortunately, infidelity is one of the leading causes of divorce. Unfortunately, many Christian marriages end in divorce than the rest of the population of non-Christian marriages around the globe. This proves that it takes more work for the Christian marriage to stay together and connected in order to keep it together, because the devil targets against the Christian marriage more so than non-Christian marriages. He does this because the Christian marriage is covered by God and is a threat against his evil kingdom—you two being an inspiration to other married couples, you two working together in unity in the church or in ministry, and you two building a firm foundation of love and a spirit filled household and relationship.

In order for it to be Christ-like centered, rewarding, and fulfilling, God must be the center of the Christian marriage at all times. When Christ is the center, in times like this, it would take Christ to help you choose to stay in-spite of, and work the relationship out until the union is back bonded again.

A Scenario that Happens All Over the World:

Scenario 1:

Brian has never had a need or longed to be with anyone else other than his wife Stacy of fifteen years with their two young kids. Their relationship was never haunted by any woman or man wanting either of them. As time went by within the fifteen-year span of their marriage, Stacy became ill and could not fulfill him sexually for a long while. This illness went on for well over five years and during those five years, Brian began to hang out with friends at a local bar while later snuggling at home with Stacy became harder and harder.

One weekend Kim, a new associate from work, as all of his friends worked together, went to the bar and had drinks. He and Kim began to converse more than the others as one thing led to another. The night ended with Brian waking up the next morning in Kim's bed. He had gotten caught up in the moment and had forgotten all about Stacy at home.

As he came through the front door trying to find a good alibi, Stacy was already on to his late arrival. She quickly questioned him as he quickly said he did a stay over all night at work. Somehow, Stacy bought the alibi and made breakfast for the both of them.

As time went on, Brian was staying out more and more until one day, Stacy had taken Brian's clothing to the cleaners and as she cleaned out his pockets, she discovered lipstick and a condom in his pants pocket. Later on that night, she questioned him and a huge argument burst out as she accused him of cheating. Brian yelled back in defense and stormed out of the house as if to be innocent.

As he arrived over Kim's house, he told her all about the argument and that he did not want to continue cheating on Stacy. Kim wasn't having that and began to cry and throw things at him. Brian told her that he wished that he could have them both. Kim reluctantly agreed. She would do anything to keep him.

Brian later came home after work the next day and admitted to Stacy that he had been in a relationship with

Kim and stated that he was moving out and that if she wanted him, she would have to take the both of them. His words were, "I need to tell you something, I've been having an affair and I want the both of you. If I cannot have it this way, then I want out of the relationship." He could not take the lack of love, affection, and attention that Stacy was not giving. Stacy was appalled at his request and quickly told him that he could not have his cake and eat it too. He would have to choose either her or the other woman. She also stated that it would bring shame on the kids and asked him had he thought about them and what would they think? Brian still insisted and did not change his answer, and left moving out of the house. He continued to see Kim as he often came home to be with Stacy too.

The question is, why wasn't Brian faithful to Stacy in-spite of her illness? Why didn't he support her and pray with her to get well? Why didn't he take her to get a second opinion for her illness? Why did Brian only think of himself? Do you think Stacy will get a divorce or fall and do what Brian is asking to be with both women? What happens with Kim? What do you think happens next? Put your imagination to test. How would you have handled the moment if this were you in this same position, either as Brian, Stacy, or Kim, or as them all? Why? And how? Write your answers below and if you are in a group, talk about it with them.

The Pain of Infidelity

CHAPTER 22
Issue of Communication

Issues always come when there is lack of communication. Communication is a power tool to change the world and to bring either dis-unity to a relationship, or unity to a relationship.

Dis-unity in a relationship happens when the connection of communication is lost or is not practiced. Communication must happen as often as possible within the relationship. There cannot be anything hidden. There is no communication that is unnecessary. It is necessary to communicate. When communication is effectively practiced on a daily basis, it will make your relationship and marriage stronger as the day goes by. It will also allow the stamp of understanding, agreement, and union to be approved.

Lack of communication brings unbearable arguments that can lead to separation if not handled. Many couples take it for granted that not knowing where your spouse is, is not a big deal, when in fact it is. For example, if you know that your spouse is at work, you do not need to call them throughout the day, all day and make sure they are there. This is control, possessiveness, and insecurity. There is a difference. Communication <u>has nothing</u> to do with control, possessiveness, and insecurity. Control is a sign of insecurity. All I am stating is that you should communicate about everything that you two need in order to make your relationship last, be strong, peaceful, and happy. You do not need to control their every move. This will become old and will bring an unhappy spouse and marriage. If you are guilty of this, you should concentrate on respecting your spouse's time when you two are away from each other, and trust that they are where they say they are and doing what they say they are doing.

Union/Unity comes when you two are in total agreement. He knows where you are going, and you know where he is going. You two have that understanding. Your agenda becomes his and his become yours. I am certainly not stating that he or she should know your every move, but I am stating that they should come close. There is an accountability within every marriage and communication is one of them. It is important to know where your spouse is. However, after knowing, you should not wear them out with calling them every minute with a bunch of negative accusations and questions or following them. Union/unity comes with trust, and if you want a long lasting, happy marriage and relationship, you should practice this everyday. I also talk about this in Chapter 22, The Popularity of Divorce: *Breaking the Repeated Curse*.

Issue of Communication

It is important to communicate within the single's relationships who are preparing for marriage. This is where it should begin. This is teaching you the routine that will make or break your relationship in the future when you make the choice to marry.

The issue of Communication is not only for the married couple, it is also for the entire family. You must communicate with your spouse and your child or children. I have witnessed some married couples who are so caught up in each other that they forget all about the child or children. They do not love, show attention, spend time, show affection, take care of their needs, or even care about their schooling (grades, conduct, extracurricular activities—sports, dancing, band, theater contests, etc.). Nothing matters but their significant other. So, in this case, the child or children are neglected until something bad happens and the parent has to deal with the tragedy of the matter; when it all could have been avoided if the parent had loved, showed affection, spent time, taken care of their needs, and even showed that they cared about the child's schooling. You may ask, *"what if I am not married although I have a boyfriend/ girlfriend?"* I will still say the same to you. This is even for single parents. It is important to take care of the needs of your child or children because if you do not, they will venture off and find someone or something else that will. They can come in the form of suicide, gangs, drug lords, crime, drugs, penitentiary, stealing, constantly in and out of jail, sexual relationships and sexual promiscuity, no confidence in their future, isolation-stay stuck in their rooms with no desire to come out, etc..

While there is no perfect parent or spouse, you should strive to be the best and to do your best and God will do the rest. Your best goes a long way. It really does count, even when you do not think it does.

Scenario 1:

Melissa works a double shift at night and during the day. She leaves her sixteen-year-old son and fourteen-year-old daughter at home while she works at night and leaves to go back to work in the late morning right after the kids leave for school.

It is obvious that leaving a sixteen and a fourteen-year-old home alone is a hard thing and it is important to have constant communication with them. It would be judging if one would say that she shouldn't be working a double shift because being a single mother as Melissa is, she has to do what she has to do to make ends meet. She is on housing and receives government assistance. She's doing the best she can.

Melissa gets so caught up at work that she sometimes forget to communicate and check on the kids. Things seem okay as Melissa puts too much trust in her sixteen-year-old son to do right, protect the house, and see about his sister, that she is confident that nothing will happen to them.

Until one afternoon, she receives a call that her sixteen-year-old son was caught stealing out of a grocery store

Issue of Communication

because he was hungry and claims that he and his fourteen-year-old sister was hungry and did not have any food to eat at home. He told the police that he tried to tell his mother that they were hungry and did not have any food to eat, but she was so caught up at work that she hardly ever called and communicated with them and checked up on them.

To add fuel to the fire, Melissa finds out later that her fourteen-year-old daughter is failing her grades and looks like she'll have to either retain the ninth grade or have to go to summer school. And, to make matters worse, the dance coach put her off the dance team due to failing grades and fighting.

Melissa panics and reluctantly quits her night job looking to be in a worse position financially but know it was best to communicate and to be available to see after her kids.

The question is, why did Melissa get so caught up with her job that she stopped communicating with her children? Why did she trust leaving them at home at night in the first place, considering they were teenagers? Did she make the right decision or did she do what she had to do? Why didn't Melissa help her sixteen-year-old son get a job to help her so she would not have to work at night? Why didn't her sixteen-year-old son know better not to steal from a store? Was he right in doing so? Why didn't Melissa check on her fourteen-year-old daughter's grades on a regular basis? This might have prevented her daughter from potentially having to retain the ninth grade and fighting. Why wasn't Melissa active in her daughter's school academics and extra-curricular activities, and before the disappointing results occurred? What do you think happens next? Put your imagination to test. How would you have handled the moment if this were you in this same position, either as Melissa, her son, or her daughter, or as them all? Why? And how? Write your answers below and if you are in a group, talk about it with them.

Issue of Communication

Issue of Communication

CHAPTER 23
Anger Hidden Behind Your Hands: *Breaking the Curse*

If a person holds their hands up in front of their face with their fingers pressed together, put them close in front of their eyes, there is no possible way you can see through them nor their eyes. It takes one person watching and the other person doing the exercise to see what I am talking about. You two try it...

Now that you have tried it, can you see their eyes through their hands? If you have done this exercise correctly, you should not be able to. As you cannot see behind their hands or the face of the one holding their hands in front of their face, it is the same as not being able to see the curse of anger that is secretly hidden on the inside. This is the same as saying, a pretty face is beautiful on the outside, but if you open up the inside, it may look very ugly with what may secretly be hidden.

Couples within marriages look like the ugly faced person on the inside when you hold things that hinder your spouse or fiancé from being happy. Also, when you are not honest about everything whether past or present. You should ask yourself, "should I be totally honest?" The answer is, yes. You should be totally honest to a degree of what will help your marriage and relationship to grow, and where both parties are happy. Every single thing belongs to God.

Communication is the key to having a strong long life relationship that is not easily broken. When you are angry about something, you should share it right away without holding it for days, weeks, months, and or even years. The longer you hold anger, the more it builds up within, until one day it will all burst; and to see the outcome is unbearable to watch.

Trying to hide anger is a dangerous thing. As you may think that no one can see your anger, you are wrong, they can. Anger is very hard to hide. It can be spotted from a mile away.

There are many factors that stem from anger. Look below to see if you fit one of these and place a check beside the one that applies to you:

1. Physical Abuse _____
2. Sexual Abuse _____
3. Verbal Abuse _____
4. Emotional Abuse _____
5. Spousal Abuse _____
6. Child Abuse _____
7. Environmental Abuse _____
8. Domestic Violence _____
9. Rejection _____
10. Fear _____
11. Pride _____
12. Hatred _____
13. Poverty _____
14. Hardship _____
15. Insecurity _____
16. Selfishness _____

Anger Hidden Behind Your Hands

17. Victim of Infidelity _____   **19.** Sickness _____

18. Relationship Battles _____   **20.** Jealousy _____

After you have checked the one(s) that apply to you above, share your thoughts on the lines below on what you have checked and why. Why are you carrying this anger? Who hurt you? Why are you angry about the one or ones you have checked? Have you released the anger? Have you spoken to the one or ones who hurt you and made you angry? I challenge you to release your anger on the lines below.

Now that you have shared on the lines above, know that releasing your anger can and will save yourself and your marriage, and will bring peace and harmony within your life and relationship. This also applies to the singles and those contemplating marriage.

Many things happen to many people all across the globe. There is not one perfect being that I have ever met. We all have a past, and we all have a future. Unfortunately, some pasts are very haunting. Some are holding things from their childhood and bring them all into the marriage and/or relationship. They hide the demons for fear they may lose their spouse or one they are in relationship with, and for control to keep them under their power so they will not hurt them. You cannot control a person nor should you ever be afraid (2 Timothy 1:7).

There was a time I was counseling a couple and the husband kept bringing up the fact that his wife does not do like his mother, therefore, she does everything wrong. And, that she was also passing this on to their son which made him and their son fight and argue all the time. He felt that his son was very lazy and never wanted to do anything. All he wanted to do was eat everything in the kitchen and play video games without responsibilities. As I listened to each of them fully, I spoke up and said to the father, *"you cannot control your wife to be like your mother nor can you control your son and throw in his face that he's just like his mother."* Then I said to the mother, *"You cannot let your son be lazy and not give him any responsibilities."* Later on in the session, the father mentioned that he had issues from his childhood and first marriage that he's not proud of which has everything to do with him not being able to trust his wife and wanting to discipline his son all the time because of the abuse he suffered. He was very angry on the inside, which is the hidden anger that I am speaking about that must be removed in order to have a happy, peaceful, and unified marriage as well as family. This is for every relationship and for the married couple who is dealing with this challenging issue. It is obvious that his issues were way deeper than his marriage, his wife, and his son. It was a must that he released his inner anger and past in order to be free and to be able to successfully love his wife, and love and rightfully discipline his son the right way instead of with abuse from the hidden inner anger.

This is the same with anyone, whether male or female, if you do not release hidden anger, it will hinder any relationship you are in.

How do you release hidden inner anger:

1. Come out of denial. Admit that you have a problem with anger.
2. Identify what you are angry about. (Go down the line beginning with childhood on up to adult. If you were married several times, deal with that as well. If you have a child or children by a first or previous marriage, deal with that until you have exalted all possibilities).

3. Release why you are angry (talk about it with either someone you can trust, with your spouse, pastor, or counselor).
4. Apologize to those you may have hurt.
5. Ask God to heal you completely and let the past go and move on with your life.
6. Walk in your freedom and peace of mind.

Breaking the Curse

Generational curses come in different ways. They usually come with a root attached to them in which could derive from generations to generations back, and can go as far back as our ancestors in slavery—pain, anger, hatred, unforgiveness, abuse, molestation, incest, rape, lust, drugs, alcohol, infidelity (adultery), and so on (Exodus 20:5).

Generational curses come in all sorts of spirits that attach themselves on the second and third generations. Most times, they become worse through time as they are handed down from generation to generation. Generally, most people do not take them as serious as they should. Some make gestures like, *"you look crazy just like yo' father."* Some even say, *"you fat just like your grandmother."* Some go much further back in time, *"Your bad attitude is way worse than your great, great grandfather who was in and out of jail for his anger."* These statements are considered as generational traits. Meaning, the son or daughter acts, or talks, or looks in a way that is just like the mother or the father who they were birthed from and/or just like someone from the family, for lack of better words, from the bloodline. However, these curses are passed down on the child without their consent and without warning from your parents or ancestors. They are passed down because of the sins of their fathers as it is spoken in the Bible in Numbers 14:18.

Below are some generational curses that are passed down.

Generational Curses:

Momma's Boy is the term often used when a mother babies and shows more attention to her son than her other children. The boy is usually spoiled and gets anything he wants. This is also a generational curse that must be stopped. No parent should favor one child over the other. By doing so, it can cause all kinds of resentments, divisions, fighting, abuse, hatred, anger, and even murder. God forbid. In some cases, the boy acts as if he cannot do without his mother and clings to her out of reason.

In the marriage, this generational curse wants its way all the time and expects the spouse to give it to him. He is very selfish and spoiled. He will even fight the spouse if she does not give him his way or treat him like his mother does. He compares everything to what his mother would do. This can hinder his marriage because it is out of order. He should cling to his wife rather than to his mother (Genesis 2:24). He can still love his mother, but should not love so much that she is all he loves and desires everything from and nobody else matters.

Momma's Girl is a term that works the same way as "Momma's Boy" as it is used when a mother babies and shows more attention to her daughter than her other children. The girl is usually very selfish and spoiled and gets anything she wants. Again, no parent should favor one child over the other. By doing so, it can cause all kinds of resentments, divisions, fighting, abuse, hatred, anger, and even murder—God forbid.

In the marriage, this generational curse wants its way all the time and expects you to give it to her. She will even fight the spouse if he does not give her her way or treat her like her mother does. She compares everything to what her mother would do. In some cases, the girl acts as if she cannot do without her mother and clings to her out of reason. This can hinder her marriage because it is out of order. She should cling to her husband rather than her mother. She can still love her mother, but should not love so much that she is all she loves and desires everything from and nobody else matters.

Momma's Boy and Momma's Girl acts in the same way as Daddy's Boy and Daddy's Girl, just the other way around. They both are still hindrances if not properly handled in order and respectfully put in their places.

Attack of Abuse comes from the other siblings, peers, and possibly even from their father or mother who is having to deal with watching the guilty parent spoil the child unreasonably. Some are never delivered from this curse until they are an adult or even of old age. Some never release. Some never forgive. They take the hurt and abuse to their grave. I would not encourage this upon anyone. I realize it is hard and is a very sensitive subject, especially if it has happened to you for a long period of time. Release is always the best option for your sake and peace.

This attack has left marriages with skeletons of murder, involuntary manslaughter, restraining orders, divorce, kidnapping, suicide, and even repercussions. There are some cases where some have been put in a mental institution because they could not deal with the residue and scars of the attack(s). You can be set free from this abuse, and live a free and peaceful life.

Drugs are another major factor of this generational curse. It is also passed down from generation to generation. You may have heard that your grandfather or grandmother, or even one of your parents were on drugs, so the poisonous seed of that drug was passed down to you.

In the marriage, this drug will do as the alcohol spirit will. It will hurt and use anyone in order to get the drug. It does not have any patience or tolerance for others. It does not care who you are nor does it care who it hurts until it is sober. It will tear up the marriage, tear up the home, verbally and physically abuse the spouse and kids (if any), and leave a legacy of financial debt due to trying to fulfill this deadly drug. A marriage cannot last with this bondage. This generational curse must be broken in order to have a successful life and marriage.

Alcohol works the same way as all the other examples. It too is a generational curse that is passed down from generation to generation. Your parents may not have dealt with this, but your grandparents or aunt or uncle has. It can come down from the bloodline.

Alcohol destroys the marriage as the husband or wife abuses the other in order to get the drug of that generational spirit or is controlled by its spell. And as a result, leaves the innocent spouse with scars and a train or abuse that is almost never recovered.

Mental Disorders are just like those mentioned above, they just carry a different spirit and struggle. Again, it is passed down from generation to generation and attaches itself unto you. Although this is not your fault as to why you received such hardship, you can still be free as if you never had it. God can take this mental stronghold away from you and heal your mind completely (1 Corinthians 2:16).

This disorder is brought into the marriage as a result of rape, abuse, and molestation. They think the husband or wife is going to hurt them just as the one who raped, abused, and/or molested them in their past.

Sexual Disorders is also a generational curse. This is why you may have heard of a person who cannot abstain him or herself from sexual contact very long, and some cannot abstain at all. They feel that they got to have it all the time. This disorder, which is a spirit, gives them a strong desire that is most times too hard for them to abstain.

This is true in the marriage. This is why you may have heard or encountered a spouse who just cannot stop sleeping with other men or women. Or have multiple children by different men or women. This is considered a disorder when you cannot stop on your own.

Fear is another generational curse although there are many. It is also passed down from generation to generation, which brings torment. Fear brings torment. It will make you afraid and intimidated of everybody and everything; even things that are not true or real. It will make you hallucinate, dream bad dreams, or have negative visions. In marriage, it will make you afraid to make your spouse mad, it will make you shun away from their love and affection in thinking they will hurt and take advantage of you. Fear also makes you reject your spouse and keeps you two from getting on one accord and staying unified. It puts you in a box and keeps you there until you make a determined decision that you are no longer going to accept and receive this tormented spirit, and began to rebuke it out of your life, marriage, family, thoughts, dreams, mind, and visions.

You may wonder why you cannot get free from these curses, it is because they are a spirit and a stronghold that only God can remove (2 Corinthians 10:4-5). He can remove them through healing. Submit yourself to God and ask Him to heal you and remove the generational curse from off of your life by the Blood of Jesus Christ Who died for your very struggle to give you freedom, restoration, and healing which makes you whole and free indeed.

Scenario 1:

Bobby slammed the door in his boss's face after getting fired because he got into a fight with one co-worker and went off on another one of his co-workers. He knows Janet is going to be mad because this is the fifth time he'd been fired due to his anger in a month. It doesn't help the fact that they got bills to pay and not enough money to pay them. Janet is tired of Bobby's terrible temper and threatens that he stops getting mad and fighting and to take care of his household.

Bobby just got home and gives Janet the bad news. "I got fired again." He looks down in shame and sadness.

Her eyes widen and she begins to cry. "Bobby I don't know what I'm gon' do with you... You know we have bills, why you gon' go and do that? I can't keep taking care of you and everybody else!"

Bobby shoots back. "I don't know why I get mad, it's like it's something inside of me making me go off on people. It's like I wanna' fight and can't contain myself. My Pops had the same bad temper. He served time in jail for killing a man years back."

Janet speaks up, "I don't know what it is but we gon' go and get you some help."

The following day, Bobby and Janet walked in a counselor's office and explained what was going on with Bobby as he admitted he has a problem. The first thing that comes out of the counselor's mouth is, "Sounds like a generational curse. It's a Spiritual thing that's why you cannot stop. It will take prayer, practice, and discipline. But *you have done the first step by admitting that you have a problem."*

The question is, should Janet be mad at Bobby for his anger and the fact that he can't keep a job because of his anger? Should Janet kick Bobby out until he get himself together? Why did Bobby and Janet wait to get help after getting fired? Who did Bobby get that generational curse from? Did Janet make the right decision in getting Bobby help? Was it good that Bobby made the first step by admitting that he has a problem? What do you think happens next? Put your imagination to test. How would you have handled the moment if this were you in this same position, either as Bobby or Janet, or as them both? Why? And how? Write your answers below and if you are in a group, talk about it with them.

Anger Hidden Behind Your Hands

CHAPTER 24
Mind over Matter

The definition of *mind over matter* means the use of will power to overcome physical problems. It is used to imply that the mind has the power to control the body and physical environment around them.

Mind over matter has the power to stay calm in most hostile situations. It is the ability to stay quiet before jumping into conclusions and running off at the mouth. Society is filled with people and situations that will test you to use your mouth in a negative way. They will cause you to lose control and make matters worse than they should had you stayed calm. By staying calm and listening before you speak, you then control the situation, the atmosphere, the conversation, the problem at hand, and you do not let it get the best of you.

In a marriage, it is important to stay calm with your spouse during trying times and heated arguments. You have to use your mind by not allowing them to make you do or say something that you live to regret. Mind over matter comes when you have complete control over the situation and that you do not allow the other(s) to make you succumb to their bad attitude and/or attacks.

Mind over matter makes you think before speaking or reacting. What this means is that you give the situation a chance for a positive outcome, rather than something negative and out of control.

Scenario 1:

Cedric and John have been friends for well over six years. They met in junior high on into high school. Their parents also know one another. They all often go out and spend time together.

One day Cedric pulled up to a pump at a gas station while John and his family followed not too far behind. Cedric proceeds to get out of his SUV as another car speeds to the opposite pump directly on side of him, a guy jumps out and snatches Cedric's pump instead of using the pump that is located right next to his own car. It was a fast, weird situation and one that caused Cedric to stay calm and not allow his anger and actions to get the best of him. He used his mind over the current matter that was before him. His first reaction was to snatch the pump handle back from the guy, but instead he stepped back and waited for the guy to get done, drive off, and then he proceeded to use the same pump.

You may ask why didn't Cedric just go to another pump? Well, that was not the answer over the matter. The test came to make Cedric blow up and begin fighting the guy as John would run over and jump in. One thing would have led to another and the outcome could have been more serious than expected. Cedric did not allow the guy to control him, instead Cedric controlled himself, the environment around him which may have saved his life, and the matter at hand.

The question is, can you say that you can do this same thing? Can you stay calm in this type of situation if it had ever happened to you? Has this ever happened to you? Was the other guy in the car wrong for snatching the pump from Cedric? Why do you think John was riding in the other car with Cedric's family instead of with him? Would you have lost it and began fighting the guy? Would you have gotten your friend involved? What do you think happens next? Put your imagination to test. How would you have handled the moment if this were you in this same position, either as Cedric, his family/John, or the guilty guy, or as them all? Why? And how? Write your answers below and if you are in a group, talk about it with them.

_____
_____
_____

Scenario 2:

Michelle and Darlene cleans the church every Sunday right after service is over. Often times, church members are still inside of the sanctuary talking as if they'd not planned on leaving no time soon. Michelle reluctantly and hesitantly looks at Darlene before approaching the church members to ask them to leave so she and Darlene can finish cleaning the sanctuary. "Can you all...?"

One of the sister's verbally lashes back as if she was waiting on Michelle to say something, "I'm still talking! You don't tell me what to do, you ain't gettin' paid to clean this place?"

Michelle stays calm and quiet as she thinks about what she's about to say. "I'm sorry sister, I don't mean to break your conversation, but we have to clean to prepare for next service. This is why we are asking you to leave out of the sanctuary."

The sister lets Darlene talk as if to be surprised that she did not lash back with her as what she was waiting for. The sister does not say yes or no, she just walks off with the other sisters as they kept talking in conversation leaving out of the sanctuary.

Michelle and Darlene went back to cleaning as if nothing happened.

The question is, can you say that you can do this same thing? Can you stay calm in this type of situation if it had ever happened to you? Has this ever happened to you? Was the sister wrong for lashing out at Michelle? Should Michelle had given the sister a piece of her mind and began yelling at her in the sanctuary? Should Darlene had jumped in? Did Michelle use mind or matter in this situation? What do you think happens next? Put your imagination to test. How would you have handled the moment if this were you in this same position, either as Michelle, Darlene, or the guilty sister, or as them all? Why? And how? Write your answers below and if you are in a group, talk about it with them.

Mind over Matter

Scenario 3:

Monique always shop at a local grocery store and never has any problems. After she'd gotten all of her groceries, she had a taste for some ice cream and saw a sign stating that they were on sale—two for the price of one. She picked up two of them.

As she approached the checkout counter, placed her groceries on the conveyor belt, she proceeded to ask the cashier "is the sale true?" Just as Monique asked the cashier the question, the store manager comes over and yells, "I don't know anything about a sale, if you didn't hear it from me, it ain't true!" His unexpected, terrible attitude was very shocking and out of control which caused Monique, the cashier, and others to look very surprised.

Monique kept quiet at first but wanted so badly to give him a peace of her mind. Well, it didn't work for long. She yelled back at the store manager as he kept talking and picking at her as if to have a vendetta against her. It was worse that she did not even know him. He shoots back at her, "If you don't like how I'm talking to you, you can leave the store!" Everybody standing around is still looking and is shocked and Monique is embarrassed but very upset.

She knew she was innocent and the fact that she let the store manager get the best of her and made her yell back, made her more upset at herself. She did not have mind over matter. *She did not take control over the matter and not allow the matter to control her. Instead, she allowed the matter to control her and she lost it.*

She finally left the store after giving him a piece of her mind and a couple of other things that she later regretted.

The question is, what made the store manager go off on Monique? Do you think it was necessary for him too? Why didn't another manager or employee jump in and help? Was Monique successful at taking control over the matter? What could she have done differently and more effectively? What do you think happens next? Put your imagination to test. How would you have handled the moment if this were you in this same position, either as Monique, the cashier, or the store manager, or as them all? Why? And how? Write your answers below and if you are in a group, talk about it with them.

_____

_____

_____

_____

_____

_____

_____

_____

Mind over matter works in every relationship and in every matter. It is the power to overcome challenges that you, your spouse, and/or family may face. Challenges are successful when you do not allow them to overtake you two, but you two overtake the challenges. It is staying calm in every situation and not allowing the other to get to you. I will admit, it is quite challenging but can be conquered as Cedric and Michelle did. This should be your goal the win in every area of your life if you ever encounter a challenging situation. Your challenging situation can come in the form of the nagging child or children, nagging spouse, and the nagging stress of things outside of your marriage. The challenge or stress will press you to bring this into the relationship, as well as the family; and lose it. The goal is not to allow things and people to make you lose control over any matter that come your way on a daily basis.

25
CHAPTER
Christ's Love for Us

You can never know Christ's love for you as well as for us all. He created the Heavens and the earth, called us to live in harmony, and multiply. God had great things planned for His people. Unfortunately, things changed due to disobedience and those plans were hindered. The good news came as something awesome happened as God took what seem like an un-changing decision, and sent His darling Son Jesus Christ to earth to die for our sins so that we may have eternal life.

As I share that, I share it to say that just as He has loved us then, He loves us now. He is unchanging. So therefore, His love for His people is one that cannot not be described nor duplicated. He loves you and every person you love and care about as well. This means, He cares about your relationship. He cares about your marriage. He cares about your life. He cares about what you care about. He cares about whatever you are troubled about and He cares about what you are happy with.

Jesus should be the center of your relationship and marriage. You can never afford to leave Him out. Chaos and calamity happens when He is left out. Confusion and the door opens to all kinds of wrong when Jesus is left out. Make today the day that you choose to make Jesus Christ the center of your relationship, marriage, and life.

This is the chapter to remember the Lord thy God and His love for you, your spouse, and your children (if any). It is a call to bring Him into your marriage if you have not already. You cannot afford not to. So with that said, whatever you are going through within you relationship, just know that you can count on God's love to fix it and make it right.

Winning Together comes to win in the marital relationship. Although there is no perfect marriage or relationship, *Winning Together* encourages the Christian Believer to strive for perfection while perfecting those challenging areas in your life and relationship that come to hinder.

Emotional Needs Evaluation Chart & Check

Rate <u>your</u> emotional needs <u>towards your spouse</u> below by marking your score on the line. Total your score at the end to see how you rate in this area for improvement, if needed. You can also complete the charts if you are single, contemplating marriage in the future, as it prepares you to work on these specific areas, if needed.

Positive Attitude

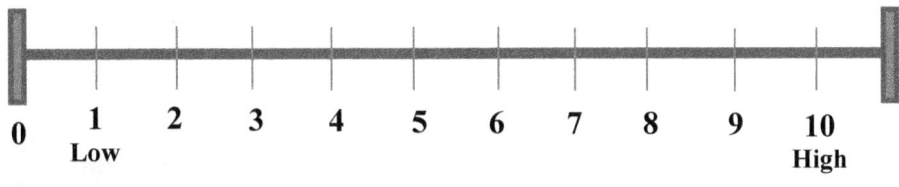

Mark Score Here _____

Sexual Desire

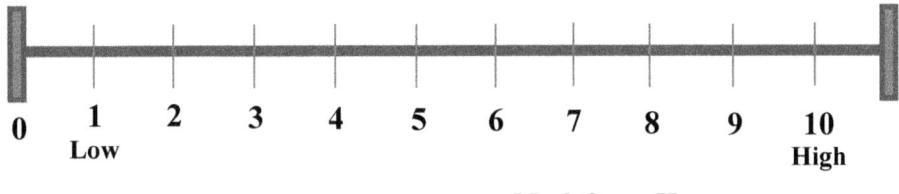

Mark Score Here _____

Bad Habits

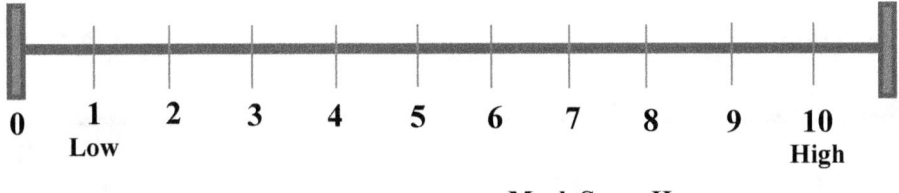

Mark Score Here _____

Emotional Needs Evaluation Chart & Check (con't.)

Communication

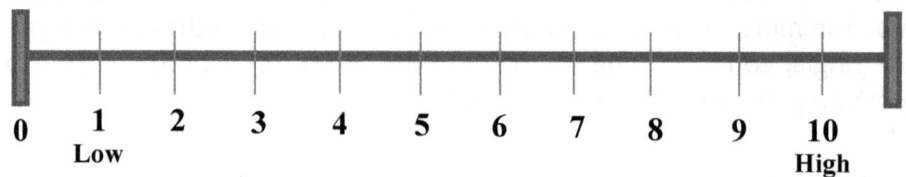

Mark Score Here _____

Need for Affection

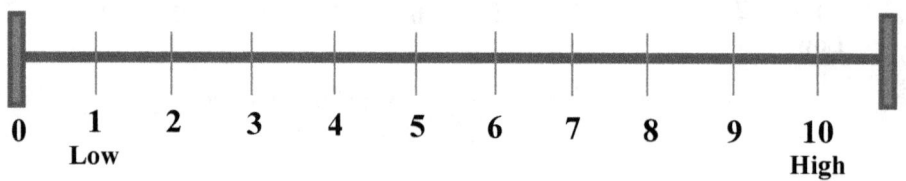

Mark Score Here _____

Financial Support

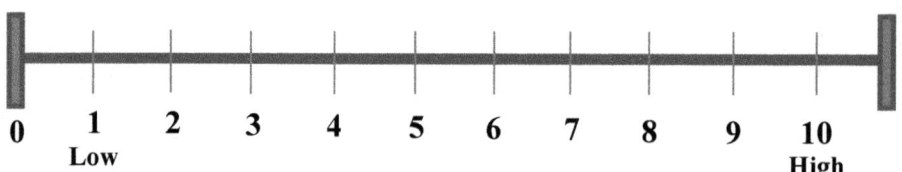

Mark Score Here _____

Attraction

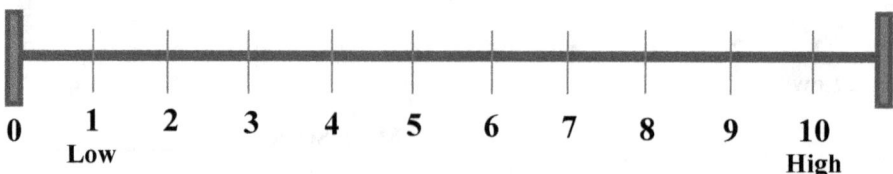

Mark Score Here _____

Emotional Needs Evaluation Chart & Check (con't.)

Aim to Please Sexually

```
0   1   2   3   4   5   6   7   8   9   10
    Low                                 High
```

Mark Score Here _____

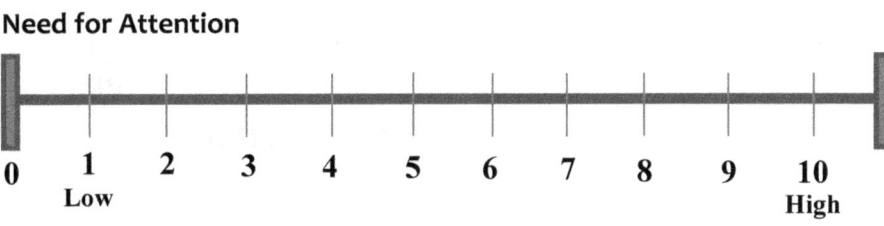

Need for Attention

```
0   1   2   3   4   5   6   7   8   9   10
    Low                                 High
```

Mark Score Here _____

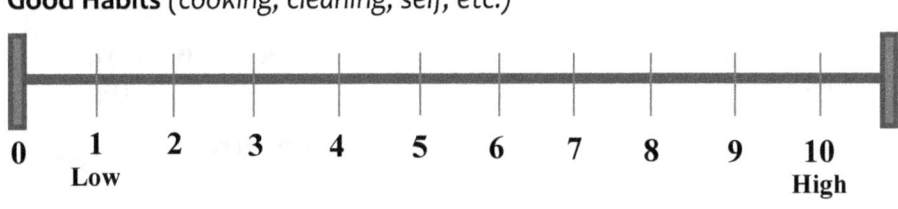

Good Habits (cooking, cleaning, self, etc.)

```
0   1   2   3   4   5   6   7   8   9   10
    Low                                 High
```

Mark Score Here _____

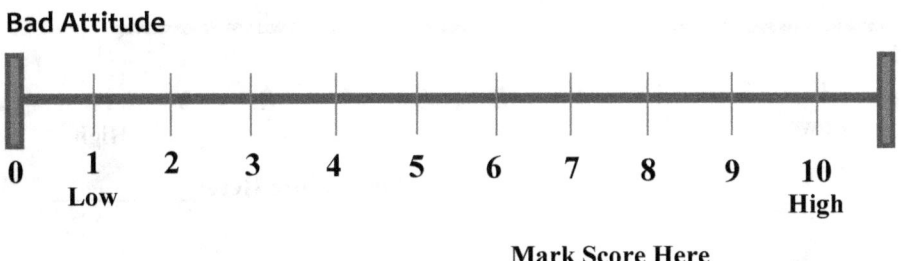

Bad Attitude

```
0   1   2   3   4   5   6   7   8   9   10
    Low                                 High
```

Mark Score Here _____

Her Hobbies His Hobbies Evaluation Chart & Check

Check the hobbies that apply to you of what <u>you do with your spouse</u> below and total your score at the end to see how you rate in this area for improvement, if needed. You can also complete the charts if you are single, contemplating marriage in the future, as it prepares you to work on these specific areas, if needed.

Watch TV

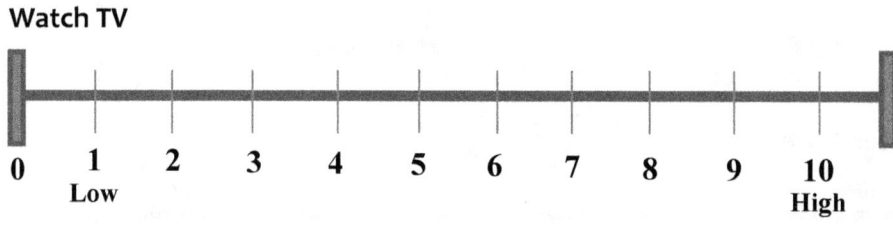

Mark Score Here _____

Rent Movies

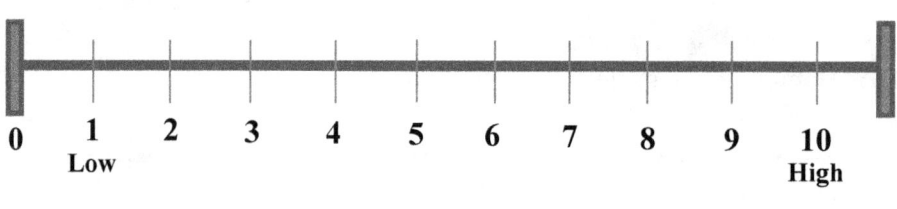

Mark Score Here _____

Exercise

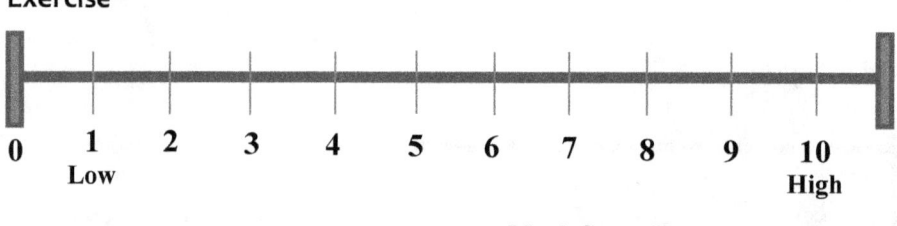

Mark Score Here _____

Mark Your Total Score Below

Below is time to total up your scores from each of the charts above. Please mark your totals below.

Emotional Needs Evaluation Chart & Check

    Positive Attitude _____
    Sexual Desire _____
    Bad Habits _____
    Communication _____
    Need for Affection _____
    Financial Support _____
    Attraction _____
    Aim to Please Sexually _____
    Need for Attention _____
    Good Habits _____
    Bad Attitude _____

Her Hobbies His Hobbies Evaluation Chart & Check

    Watch TV _____
    Rent Movies _____
    Exercise _____

Grand Total _____

After totaling up your results, now write the areas you need to work on:

_____

_____

_____

_____

Now that you have marked your totals on the lines from the previous page and have written down those areas you need to work on above, you can now see where you are with your relationship(s) with your spouse. These charts are not given to embarrass you if your scores are low, they are to help and encourage you to perfect those areas that are lacking in low scores, and bring them up to high scores.

You can do the charts repeatedly after you go and perfect those areas, and come back to this book and do them again until you get the high scores need. Your scores not only will be higher, but you will increase a high score in your relationship.

These charts will help you in more ways than you know. At times, you may think that you know your spouse but may lack in some of these areas. This is normal because we as humans are not perfect. However, what makes you awesome is that, although your score may not be a 10 on each chart, you are willing and strive to make the change(s) in those areas in order to become a 10. Your spouse is counting on you, and so am I. You can be the best spouse, family, and individual on this planet earth. I am rooting for you!

GROUP SESSION

DATE: _____
NAME: _____
MARRIED OR SINGLE? _____
DO YOU HAVE A CHILD OR CHILDREN? _____
   IF YES, HOW MANY? _____
PLACE OF SESSION: _____
NAME OF SESSION: _____
NAME OF LEADER/TEACHER/INSTRUCTOR: _____

CHAPTER(S) YOU ARE USING FOR GROUP SESSION _____

_____
_____
_____
_____
_____

SCENARIO(S) IN THE BOOK YOU ARE USING FOR SESSION _____

_____
_____
_____
_____
_____

AREA(S) OF CONCERN _____

_____
_____
_____

GROUP SESSION con't.

LIKES *(WHAT MADE YOU FALL IN LOVE & WHAT YOU LIKE NOW)* _____

_____
_____
_____
_____
_____
_____
_____

DISLIKES *(PET PEEVES- WHAT ANNOYS YOU)* _____

_____
_____
_____
_____
_____
_____
_____

BAD HABITS

_____
_____
_____
_____
_____

HOW HE MAKES ME FEEL _____

_____
_____

GROUP SESSION con't.

HOW SHE MAKES ME FEEL

ROMANTIC IDEAS *(WHAT TURNS HIM OR HER ON?)*

WHAT ARE YOU WILLING TO COMPROMISE IN THOSE AREAS OF CONTROL? HOW?

GROUP SESSION con't.

WHAT ARE YOUR SPOUSE'S GOALS & PLANS IN LIFE? _____

_____
_____
_____
_____
_____

WHAT DO YOU TWO HAVE IN COMMON? _____

_____
_____
_____
_____
_____
_____

WHAT DO YOU LIKE MOST ABOUT YOUR SPOUSE? _____

_____
_____
_____
_____
_____
_____

ARE YOU FULFILLED SEXUALLY? IF NOT, NAME THE REASONS. _____

_____
_____

GROUP SESSION con't.

IS ROMANCE A PLUS OR A NEGATIVE IN YOUR RELATIONSHIP? WHY OR WHY NOT?

IS AFFECTION A PLUS OR A NEGATIVE IN YOUR RELATIONSHIP? WHY OR WHY NOT?

DO YOU SPEND TIME WITH YOUR SPOUSE? IF SO, WHAT DO YOU DO?

GROUP SESSION con't.

_____
_____
_____
_____
_____
_____

NAME AREAS OF CONCERN FOR YOUR CHILD/CHILDREN _____

_____
_____
_____
_____
_____
_____

CIRCLE WHO YOU ARE NOW

Loving	Controlling	Compromisable
Hateful	Demand respect	Family man
Selfish	all the time	Family woman
Egotistical	Over barring	Spend time with
Stubborn	Possessive	the child/children
Very romantic	Smart-aleck	Like to be alone
Affectionate	Unfaithful	Intricate
Like your own way	Faithful	Motivator

HAVE A GROUP DICUSSION ABOUT WHAT YOU CIRCLED ABOVE. ADD NOTES HERE_____

_____
_____
_____
_____

ADDITIONAL GROUP SESSION SPACE

ADDITIONAL GROUP SESSION con't.

ADDITIONAL GROUP SESSION con't.

ADDITIONAL GROUP SESSION con't.

ADDITIONAL GROUP SESSION con't.

ADDITIONAL GROUP SESSION *con't.*

ADDITIONAL GROUP SESSION con't.

ADDITIONAL GROUP SESSION con't.

Index:

1. **Chapter 5:** Wikipedia, the free encyclopedia: (especially of a separated or unmarried couple) share the duties of parenting (a child). http://en.wikipedia.org/wiki/Coparenting (p.55)

2. **Chapter 4:** Family Time Builds the Bridge & Keeps it Standing
   Bullying: http://nobullying.com/bullying-statistics/ (p. 38)
   School Shootings: http://www.stoptheshootings.org/ (p. 38)
   Children & Teen suicide:
   http://jasonfoundation.com/prp/facts/youth-suicide-statistics/ (p. 40)

   Teen Substance Abuse: https://www.teentreatmentcenter.com (p. 40)

   http://www.inspirationsyouth.com/statistics-teen-drug-use-abuse-addiction/ (p. 40)

3. **Chapter 13:** Victoria's Secret, https://www.victoriassecret.com (p. 168).

4. **Chapter 13:** Bath and Body Works, http://www.bathandbodyworks.com (p. 168-169)

5. **Chapter 23:** Springer Show, http://www.jerryspringertv.com/ (p. 245)

6. **Chapter 23:** The Pain of Infidelity
   http://thegospelcoalition.org/article/factchecker-divorce-rate-among-christians/ (p. 281)

Winning Scriptures From the Book:

CHAPTER 3
Galatians 6:7, Job 4:8,
Genesis 2:24,
Proverbs 22:6,
Genesis 2:24,
Psalms 91,

2 Corinthians 10:5,
Ecclesiastes 5:6,
Psalms 133:1,
James 1:19,
John 10:10

CHAPTER 4
Hebrews 13:4

Genesis 2:23

CHAPTER 5
Proverbs 3:5-6

CHAPTER 6
2 Corinthians 10:4-5
Exodus 20:14

Matthew 18:21-22
Isaiah 53:4-5

CHAPTER 9
Hebrews 13:4

CHAPTER 10
Hebrews 13:4

CHAPTER 12
Hebrews 13:4

CHAPTER 13
Hebrews 13:4
1 Corinthians 7:7-8

1 John 4:1
1 Corinthians 7:4

CHAPTER 14
Hebrews 13:4

Genesis 27-28

CHAPTER 16
John 15:1-7 (Emp. on 1,4,5)

John 15:1,4,5

CHAPTER 18
1 Corinthians 14:33
Acts 3:19
Isaiah 53:5
Isaiah 40:31

John 8:36
2 Peter 3:17
Colossians 1:14
Matthew 18:21-22

CHAPTER 19
Ephesians 5:23
Philemon 1:6
Colossians 4:2
Proverbs 18:10

Galasians 5:17
Proverbs 16:19, 29:23
Matthew 12:25

CHAPTER 20
Genesis 2:23
Galatians 5:17

Philippians 1:6
Matthew 19:6

CHAPTER 21
Matthew 19:9
James 5:16

Matthew 18:21-22

CHAPTER 22
2 Timothy 1:7
Exodus 20:25
Numbers 14:18

1 Corinthians 2:16
2 Corinthians 10:4-5

CHAPTER 23
Genesis 2:23
Galatians 5:17
Genesis 2:24

Philippians 1:6
Matthew 19:6

OTHER BOOKS BY STEPHANIE

1. When Ramona Got Her Groove Back from God
2. My Song of Solomon
3. My Song of Solomon *Prayer Journal*
4. Position Your Faith for Great Success
5. Position Your Faith for Great Success *Workbook*
6. The Purpose Chaser: *For Children Ages 5 to 12*
7. God Loves *Thugs* Too!
8. The Locker Room Experience: *For the Struggling Athlete & Coach, & Tips on How to Get Recruited in Sports*
9. Church Hurt: *How to Heal & Overcome It*
10. Winning Together: *His Needs Matter, Her Needs Are Important*
11. Winning Together As a Parent
12. The Power of Healing
13. The Power of the Holy Spirit
14. RE*shape* YOU: *A Fitness Guide to Teach YOU How to Create the NEW YOU from the Inside Out*

You may purchase them at any Christian Bookstore and anywhere books are sold.

CONTACT

For bookings for booksignings, speaking engagements, group siminars/sessions, or ordering books, etc.:

STEPHANIE FRANKLIN
STEPHANIE FRANKLIN MINISTRIES
PO BOX 682532
HOUSTON, TX 77268

EMAIL: info@stephaniefranklinministries.org
WEBSITE: www.stephaniefranklin.org

Stephanie Franklin, M.A. (T.S.)

Obtains a Master of Arts Degree in Theological Studies and has a vision to reach the world with her mentoring, teaching, life coaching, and preaching ministry. She has a heart to reach the youth and young adults along with the entire family, bringing them all together as a unified fold. One of her greatest desires is to be used by God in whatever capacity He chooses.